This book
Adelaide Qu

NEW LIVES

New Lives

*What Happened When Twenty-Two
Ordinary People Encountered
the Extraordinary Love of God*

Edited by
Bob Ovies

SERVANT BOOKS
Ann Arbor, Michigan

Published by Servant Books
       P.O. Box 8617
       Ann Arbor, Michigan 48107

Cover photo copyright © H. Armstrong Roberts
Book Design by John B. Leidy

Scripture texts used in this work are taken from the NEW
AMERICAN BIBLE copyright © 1970 by the Confraternity of
Christian Doctrine, Washington, D.C., all rights reserved, and
from THE LIVING BIBLE, copyright © 1971 by Tyndale House
Publishers, Wheaton, Illinois, all rights reserved.

Printed in the United States of America
ISBN 0-89283-077-8

To Mark

Contents

Preface

"For you have a new life. It was not passed on to you from your parents, for the life they gave you will fade away. This new one will last forever, for it comes from Christ" (1 Pt 1:23).

TWELVE YEARS AGO my wife Kathy and I had our first child, a boy named Mark. He seemed so healthy and happy that he made us sure of our own health and happiness. Yet three months later he died.

Mark was a "crib death;" his death happened without warning or explanation.

The grief and confusion and anger we felt in those days seemed total, and completely untouched by all the friends and family who tried so hard to share it and alleviate it.

For the first time in my life I recognized my own insufficiency. I had always thought that I possessed a great reservoir of inner strength, but there, in that place so close to death, I realized that my strength had evaporated. I was so powerless and vulnerable and unable to hold on to life that it stunned me.

I also realized that I wasn't at all sure that God would help me. I had always believed in God, but now I was frightened of "letting go," afraid to trust that he'd really hold me together.

I felt like I was about to enter a pitch black room. I didn't want to go in, but I had no strength to resist. In that room I would have to "let go." I would have to give up all my dreams for Mark and so many of my dreams for Kathy and myself. I would have to lie down and rest, but what would happen to me then? What if I just fell through the floor and kept falling? If I had no strength left to hold onto myself, and if God wasn't really going to be there to support me, I felt I might just drop forever, never touching ground, and all the while becoming horribly diminished.

Most of all, I knew that if I felt that happening, I would never hope in God again. It was that hopelessness that I feared more than anything else.

As I look back on that time, I know that it was one of the most priceless of my life, even though I entered it exhausted, angry, and afraid. What I discovered in that "room," and in that "letting go," is that Jesus Christ is a real person, one we can trust totally. He is not just an historical moral leader; he is alive today, and it's safe to depend on him because he responds to us in a personal, powerful, and real way.

As I began to trust him, I found that the room that had looked so dark was flooded with light. The floor was not only solid, it was piled high with gifts. In letting go of everything, Kathy and I had discovered a whole new life.

God gave us many "little" gifts. Questioning whether God really knew or cared about who our dead infant was, we opened the Bible to the words, "For upon him the Father, God himself, has set his seal." Anguishing over whether infants could know God—whether Mark could really be in heaven—Kathy saw a young boy we knew who couldn't have heard about Mark's death. He walked up and handed her a picture of an infant in a bassinet in heaven, and said, "Look what I found in the street this morning. You want it?" There were many of these little gifts, tangible gifts that we took gladly and were grateful for, and that God used to draw life out of death.

But there were bigger gifts too, experiences that are impossible to describe, yet so life-giving and so real—as real as knowing with certainty that you are loved.

In the end, we not only weren't diminished, we were somehow increased. Despite the pain, which we still carry with us to some degree, the presence of God was so real and so healing that we found even greater hope and faith. We were more certain of our day-by-day relationship with God and with each other than ever before.

Since that time, we've seen God touch and profoundly change the lives of hundreds of people that we know. Jesus not only prevents people from being destroyed, he gives them beautiful new lives. He does that with the most ordinary people. That's the miracle. That's the good news this book is meant to share. The most important discovery we can ever make is to find out with real certainty, through all the doubt, fear and scepticism that we bring to the question, that Jesus Christ's entering into ordinary lives in personal, powerful, saving ways is not extraordinary at all. It is ordinary—the most ordinary possible response from a loving and personal God.

There are twenty-two stories gathered here—brief accounts of personal encounters with Jesus.

Some people were looking for this encounter, others weren't. They came to it in various circumstances, with different problems and needs. They include a priest, husbands and homemakers, students and teachers, businessmen, laborers, mothers and fathers, sons and daughters, young and old. Someone in the book has probably lived through circumstances and difficulties similar to your own.

Please recognize that these are not extraordinary people. To view them as being extraordinary would be to miss the deepest point of the good news they have to share. They are ordinary people, all living in the same unexceptional middle-class neighborhood, all sharing their lives in the same small and certainly unremarkable church community.

They aren't blessed with extraordinary spiritual gifts; they don't possess extraordinary faith. Some of their experiences are certainly dramatic, but they are not extraordinary. They happen often—more often than you might imagine.

The very fact that these are just ordinary men and women relating common encounters with Jesus is what makes their stories good news. It is ordinary for a loving God to act in loving ways to save his people, here and now. It happens every day. Even as you read this, it's happening all around you.

In Jesus, God makes what seemed extraordinary to be ordinary. In Jesus, he makes everything new. He doesn't just rearrange life; he begins it again, brand new. He rewrites all the old definitions; authors the ordinary miracle; declares once and for all the astonishing good news that it is ordinary for each of us to live in an intimate, loving, two-way relationship with God. It's the normal human experience—the way God created us to live. He offers this life to each of us, through Jesus Christ, and he has so many beautiful ways of making this new life happen. Here are just a few of them.

"I really saw suicide as the way out. I began to believe I deserved it. I began to plan it."

Sam Lynd

Age 41, sales representative,
married 21 years, 5 children

ONE MORNING SIX years ago, I made plans for my suicide. That same afternoon I met Jesus Christ in a way that changed my whole life.

As a kid I was always urged to overachieve, so as an adult I put everything I had into my job. I was a salesman, married fifteen years with four kids, and had reached a point where my self-worth depended on how well I performed my job. I'd watch other guys make lots of money and I'd try to be like them. They seemed to have it all together. I modelled myself after so many people that I lost my own identity.

I really didn't know who I was. As I became more of an achiever on the job, and increasingly successful in a business sense, I became less of a father and husband. As a result, I started having serious problems in my life. I was a perfect set-up for what happened.

I was so aggressive at my job that I was finally

promoted to a position where the need and the pressure were the greatest. But there, for the first time, I found that all the little business tricks I'd learned didn't always work. There was also a dip in business at that time, and I thought, "Boy, six months from now this is really going to catch up to me." I was afraid to let the boss know what was happening because I was supposed to have the world by the tail. So I hid it all, even though I knew he'd find out sooner or later.

While all this was happening, my wife was hospitalized and becoming sicker and sicker with depressions, and I didn't understand why. It seemed unfair, and it scared me. For the first time in my life I started to question, not just my adequacy on the job, but my adequacy at home. After all, my wife Margie had never been depressed before we were married. I began to admit that there might be something about me that was causing all this. As a result, I began to believe a lot of negative things about myself, until finally I slid into a depressed condition. I'd never experienced serious depression before, but now I doubted everything about myself, what I was doing, where my life was headed. As things snowballed, I finally began to think that life was futile. I was sure I couldn't go on without people discovering how badly I coped with everything.

It frightened me that Margie was so sick with depressions and hospitalized, especially when I realized it could happen to me. So I hit the point where I really saw suicide as the way out. I began to believe I deserved it. I began to plan it.

It was January, and it was icy. I decided to pick a

specific point on the road where I could just drive at high speed into something. The road conditions would make it seem like an accident, and the family would get the insurance. I felt sure it would work. One morning I made my plans. Then I wandered into a restaurant, hungry. It seemed ironic even then, since I had just planned my suicide, but I was hungry and needed food.

When I sat down, I noticed that the guy sitting across the counter from me was just beaming! He said to me, "Hey! Isn't this a great day the Lord has made?" And that just totally went by me. I thought he was nuts.

"My name's Tony," he said. "What's yours?"

I told him, with all the enthusiasm of someone that's dying.

He said, "What do you do for a living?" I was almost ashamed to tell him that I was a salesman, I was feeling so bad, but I told him. And he brightened up even more. "Hey, isn't that terrific," he said, "So am I!" But he was such a contrast to me. He was so happy. "You know," he said, "I'm having the worst year I ever had, but I'm having a ball!"

By this time I was totally disarmed. I was really confused. This guy was coming from a completely different place than any I had ever been in. I just knew you couldn't have a terrible year and still be having a ball!

"I didn't always feel that way, though," he said. "I didn't feel that way until I knew the Lord."

The way he said it startled me; he really struck me hard. I thought, "This is real to him. This man talks like he really knows God." Of course I knew some things about religion. I even went to church on Sunday. We would take the kids or I would go with Margie. I'd heard people talk about God, but I had never heard anybody talk about him so personally and with so much conviction. For some reason, I was sure that this guy wasn't just talking; he really knew what he was saying.

Then he started to tell me about his life. He said, "I've had a lot of trouble. I used to think it was because I'm black, so I went to college. I did everything I could. But people still didn't respond to me. So I hated them back. But now that's all changed. Now Jesus is helping me to love people," I didn't answer, but by this time, I really wanted to hear more.

"I used to think it was a dirty deal," he said. "I was married to this girl, a beautiful lady, but she was sick all the time. I used to think, boy, that's a raw deal. I didn't think it was fair. So I tried to make up for it by just being my own cat, going out and drinking and all that kind of thing."

As he went on talking about himself and his past life, I knew that everything he said applied to me! It was an exact parallel, a duplication of my life. I was absolutely convinced, right there on the spot, that God was not only real, but that he had arranged for this man to talk to me about my life. It was obvious to me that the man really did know God and that God was using him to talk to Sam Lynd, even though the man had no idea who I was or what his words meant to me.

So I told him, "You can't imagine how much what you've said means to me and how much it applies to me. Today I made plans to kill myself." Then I let it all out. I cried. I told him everything, right there in the restaurant. I really let him know me. I told that man the truth.

When I had told him everything—about my job, my wife in the hospital, my kids, my fears, my suicide plans—he just looked into my eyes and said, "I don't think you'll do that to yourself, because Jesus loves you, and I'm going to pray for you every day." He said, "I go to church. I go to Communion every morning, and I'm going to be praying for you, and in two weeks your wife is going to be out of that hospital. I know that God will do that for you."

Then he gave me his name and phone number and said, "You call me in two weeks. And remember, Jesus loves you." Then he walked out.

When I left that restaurant, just a few minutes later, I believed God did something to me. I couldn't explain it, but I really believed that Jesus Christ was the actual, living Son of Almighty God, and that he died to save me, Sam Lynd. I was convinced he loved me so much that he made sure that man was in the restaurant to say those things to me. Jesus had made me hungry; he put me there; he got me through that door; he changed who I was. I believed in God and in Jesus, and I began to go to God through Jesus, and he saved my life.

Two weeks later to the day Margie came home from the hospital.

Over the next several years, our lives changed totally—our attitudes and values, and our relationship with one another. Jesus changed everything. I'm still in sales, but I'm also a husband and father, and I love life. My wife has been healed, and I'm closer to her and the kids than I ever thought possible. My relationship with Jesus is one of brother to brother. He's real. He knows and loves me personally, and I love him.

That's what struck me about Tony in the restaurant six years ago; he did know Jesus personally. Now I know that I do too. I thank God for it every day of my life.

"I looked back at our married life, and all the hurt and anger and hatred I felt, all the loneliness and rejection of the past eight years came out. It just overwhelmed me. I couldn't handle it."

Marge Lynd

Age 40, homemaker,
married 21 years, 5 children

AFTER SAM AND I were married for a few years, I began to suffer depressions. These weren't simply bad moods; they were like being in a pit. I would be so depressed that sometimes I couldn't talk for a day-and-a-half. All I could see was darkness. I could have been in the Garden of Eden during that time, and I would only have seen the dirt.

I suffered these depressions periodically for eight years. As a result, I was on anti-depressants most of the time. I took librium; I had shock treatments; and I took three to four valiums a day for nearly four years.

At that time, I didn't have much of a religious life. I went to church occasionally, but it was a social thing to me. I would go one week but not the next, depending on how much entertaining we had done the night before and things like that.

When my husband Sam did this big turn-around and began to believe in Jesus I thought, "Well, this is just another thing with him, like work or the buddy system or something like that; it's just one more thing to take the place of me and the kids." So I remained depressed for a long time after his conversion. In fact, I was suspicious and resentful towards it.

During this time I had to have surgery for removal of an internal growth, and Sam prayed with me for it. When they opened me up, they found that I had a cyst but that it was all shriveled up. I was relieved, of course. I do believe now that the Lord healed me. But still, there was something else that the Lord had to work out in my life. Soon after the surgery, it all became apparent.

The day came when I looked back at our married life, and all the hurt and anger and hatred I felt, all the loneliness and rejection of the past eight years came out, rushing on me and burying me. It just overwhelmed me—so much hurt and violence, so much terrible anger. I had buried all these feelings for years, and now they were all exposed, and I couldn't handle them.

I called my psychiatrist and told him I had to get away. I said I couldn't handle this anymore. He told me to see him at the hospital rather than at his office, but when I arrived, he signed me in.

I couldn't believe it! Hospitalization was the last thing I wanted. But my psychiatrist insisted, so finally I gave in. I told him that I wanted no tranquilizers of any kind, but I let him admit me.

During my stay in the hospital, I was forced into complete honesty, with all my feelings exposed, and it was then that the Lord came to me in a personal, saving way. I could finally let him in, and he saved me.

It happened on Easter weekend—Resurrection Day. I was still really angry. I remember saying, "If God really loves me, why am I in a mental institution? I don't want to be here. This is not fun!" But one of the nuns that worked at the hospital was in charge of coordinating some of the Easter services, and for Holy Thursday and Good Friday she asked me to lead a scripture service. Of course, I had no idea what to do, but I promised I'd try. I wondered why she asked me and why I ever agreed to do it, but that's how God worked.

As I told people about Jesus on that weekend— about his love, his passion and death, his loneliness and rejection—I really came to know in a whole new way that Jesus really did understand and care about me, personally. He knew me and loved me, Marge Lynd, right where I was, and he wanted to help me.

God chose that time, and that way. Suddenly he was my personal Savior, and I knew it.

I accepted Jesus as my living Savior five years ago, and I haven't suffered a single depression since. I've never taken an anti-depressant or tranquilizer, and I've suffered no withdrawals. More importantly, my whole relationship with God and with Sam and the children has changed.

Jesus is with me all the time now, every day. He's really alive. He's there when I get up in the morning and when I go to bed at night. Through the night, he's there. Now I have a personal relationship with him. It's like having a friend with me always, one I can really talk to and listen to. I know that he loves me, that he hears me and is working in my life.

Before, I never knew God in a personal way. I don't think I ever had an honest conversation with God. I just never realized that this kind of close, loving relationship was possible. Now it seems incredible to me that I didn't know about it. And now that I do know it, my life is healed.

"I've been a devout and active Catholic all my life. Yet in the last few years, my whole life has been renewed."

Paul Weber

Age 72, retired,
married 45 years, 4 children

IM AN OLD dog, seventy-two years old, and I've been a devout and active Catholic all my life. I always felt that I had a real devotion to God, and tried to carry out my religious duties without letting up. I would beat my kids out of sleeping bags on camping trips and drive forty miles to get to Mass because it was required. I went to Communion regularly. Even if I sinned, my faith remained strong and I considered myself a loyal Catholic. Yet in the last few years, my whole life has been renewed.

When I say that, I really don't mean to say there's anything totally new in me. But there is a great deepening of all the old truths. They were all there before, and I was aware of them, and I even thought I knew them. But I know now that I was just aware of them.

I suppose it's a hackneyed example, but my relationship with God, with Jesus Christ, before this renewal took place in my life a year and a half ago, was sort of like my relationship with the President. I knew a great deal about him. I had read a great deal. But I didn't really know him. Just as I had never personally met the President, so I had never personally met Jesus Christ.

My life began to change through the prayers of a neighbor when I was hospitalized with cancer. This neighbor came to the hospital and prayed for me, and I recovered. I don't like to use the word "miracle" too lightly, but I do believe that the Lord healed me. He used good surgeons and other things, but he gave me back my life in a truly remarkable recovery, one that even the doctors were amazed at.

When I returned home and began to regain my strength, my neighbor asked if I'd like to go to a prayer meeting with him. Of course I said I would, though I didn't quite know what to expect.

At the prayer meeting I was amazed to hear people speak so familiarly and lovingly about Jesus. It was "Jesus, this" and "Jesus that," words we never used to use. We were afraid to. We would always say "Christ" or "Our Lord," but it was something less familiar than "Jesus." That told me right there that something was going on that I didn't know a lot about.

At the same time, it wasn't difficult at all for me to encounter the joyfulness of the prayer meeting. A lot of people I talk to seem to have an initial problem with that, with the idea of making noise in church. The sisters used to whop kids for doing that. But I guess that if this is the good news, we ought to be spreading it with great joy, happiness, and jubilation, because it is so good.

A few weeks later, I was baptized with the Holy Spirit, and I realized that I was beginning to share in the life of the Triune God in a new way. That really rocked me. It's an awesome thing when you stop and think about it. To me, as a result of this, God has become a real Father. I rely on him. I know that he's going to lead me and protect me. And Jesus is real in my life. He's my brother, my God, my friend, and my companion, the one who leads me to the Father.

As I said, there's nothing really new to me in all this. I guess the one thing that's new is recognizing the actual influence of the Holy Spirit. He has come out of the closet. He isn't telling me anything he didn't tell me before, but it has more point and meaning now. I have just read in one of Paul's letters, "I believe that nothing can happen that will outweigh the supreme advantage of knowing Christ Jesus." And that's the whole story. That's my story too.

Now, after seventy active years, the Lord has entered my life in a new and wonderful way. My relationship with God and my fellow man has been immensely deepened. Now I can understand when I hear people say, "Accept Jesus Christ as your personal Savior." That used to sound foreign to me, but now I say, "Of sourse! That's what it's all about!"

"My priesthood took on a whole new life and meaning. I was able to fully accept Jesus as my total Lord and total life. I was freed."

Reverend Edward Belczak

Age 28, parish priest

I ARRIVED AT our parish as a deacon. Up to that time, I had spent twenty-one years of my life trying to be somebody other than Ed Belczak, because I didn't really like the person I was. When I was a kid, I had very serious acne and preferred to stay at home rather than play ball with the other kids. I never knew how to fight and so decided I was a coward. I was a hypochondriac, afraid of every possible illness, taking pills for everything. To top it off I had a speech defect—nothing major, but enough to be made fun of, even in the seminary. I was afraid to be myself. I wasn't happy with me.

During my first year as deacon, the pastor suggested that I attend a prayer meeting in Ann Arbor. He was thinking of starting one in our own parish, so I went. But I wasn't prepared for what I found.

At the meeting, there were about four-hundred people just praising God. I certainly had never experienced anything like that before. It threw me. So I stayed back against the outer wall and watched.

Even so, I went to a second meeting, again at the suggestion of the pastor. He was not only my pastor, but someone I'd known for years as a holy and scholarly man. He'd even been my spiritual director in the seminary, and I was impressed with his continued interest in this type of prayer. So I went again, but strictly as an observer. And again, I came away scratching my head.

The following year, I was ordained to the priesthood. I remained at the same church, thankful that I could stay, but I still struggled with a lot of insecurity. I was fearful and unhappy about myself. I wanted to be a good priest and tried to do the best I could, but that never seemed good enough. Looking back, I realize now that I was continually approaching religion, and my priesthood, from an intellectual standpoint. I had never really encountered the love of the Lord, at least not in the personal way that I encountered him at Lourdes two years later.

I traveled to Lourdes with a friend who was studying in Rome, and as soon as I arrived I knew I was on holy ground, despite all the paraphernalia outside. This was a holy place for me. So I decided that I was going to bathe in the water.

There were long lines, with fifteen chairs at the end of each. The chairs were the final waiting area before you were taken, in groups of fifteen, into the baths. From the chairs you were led through a curtained area where you hung your clothes on hooks. Then you were handed a blue towel-like cloth to wrap around your waist. One person at a time would walk down the steps into the bath. After that, with the water up to your waist, they'd lean you over backwards until you were totally immersed.

The closer I got, though, the more fearful I became. I wasn't just nervous. I was almost overcome with fear.

As soon as I got inside and they told me to take off my clothes, the first thing I thought was, "I'm going to get sick for sure." It suddenly hit me full force how many people had been walking there and had been immersed in that same water, and how sick so many of them were. I realized that the bath hadn't been changed for days, and the lines of people were just endless, every day, with all that sickness.

The fear was tremendous, and other fears came: fears about what would happen to me spiritually if I went through with this, fears from the past, fears about never doing anything right. I remember saying to myself, "What am I doing here? Why the heck did I come? I must be crazy! I don't want to be here!"

But deep inside I did want to be there. I really wanted to let God do what he wanted with me. So I started praying like crazy, and I stepped into the water.

As the water reached my waist and they got ready to lean me over backwards to be immersed, all I could think to pray were prayers of trust. I just said, "OK, I let go. I let this happen. I put myself totally in the Lord's hands." And then I felt the cold water close over me.

It's hard to describe what happened next, but it was the most powerful thing I'd ever experienced. A sensation of warmth moved through my entire body, from head to foot and back again. And as it moved, it left a greater sensation of love and forgiveness and freedom than I ever imagined was possible.

It was as though someone took their hand and moved it through my whole system. When it moved down it wiped everything bad away, all my fears about God, myself, others, about being sick, about the water, everything. And when it moved back up, it put love, warmth, and goodness in the place of all those other things. I came out of that water crying. I came out loved and free, filled with an overwhelming knowledge of God's love, of living in goodness, of being forgiven all my sins.

It wasn't just euphoria, either. It was the love of a person. It was God loving me and setting me free. His goodness and warmth filled me and surrounded me.

Looking back, I believe that a major part of my act of faith consisted of the willingness to experience something I had never done before: to put my trust in God and keep an open heart and mind, in spite of my fears. And the Lord blessed that. Since then he has changed me tremendously. Now he's enabled me to love him and honestly talk with him and praise him openly and naturally, things I never was able to do before.

When I returned home, one of the things I wanted to do was to attend a prayer meeting. The pastor had started one in our own parish, which I attended several times before my trip to Lourdes, though I still hadn't felt at home there.

Now it seemed the most natural place in the world for me to be. I thought, "Why didn't I come here more often before?" Whatever insight I didn't have then, I had now. My fears were gone. My hesitation had evaporated. It was just the greatest and most natural thing in the world to praise God in that prayer meeting in that way.

I had changed, and I was still being changed. My priesthood began to take on new life and meaning. I was able to accept Jesus fully as my total Lord and total life. I was freed. I began to understand all kinds of things I never understood before.

I'm not a hypochondriac anymore, either. I don't need all those pills because I don't worry about my health. God has set me free from that, too, and I feel great.

I also find myself saying, and meaning, things like, "I really thank you, Lord" and "praise you, God" all the time now. Before when I heard people say things like that, I thought they sounded phony. I couldn't believe they were natural. Now the words just come out of me; they're part of me.

The sacraments have taken on new dimensions for me, too, especially the Eucharist. I like to read the prayer that says Jesus has come to bring liberty to captives and to set prisoners free, because I know that he's done that for me.

The Lord has opened the tomb in my life. He's pulled away the rock so that the dead man can come out alive. He's split the rock so the water of life can flow out. He removed so many heavy rocks, so many burdens. Now all that water, all that Spirit, can flow out freely.

I also recognize the power of prayer in a new way. It's something we don't think about enough. But now I've seen that power. I've seen God do so much through prayer.

But the greatest gift is to be happy with who you are, to know you're loved, to understand that you're created in the Lord's own image and likeness. I know now that the kingdom of God is in me in a way that I never really understood before.

Now Jesus is Lord of my life. He's the person for whom I was created, my brother and savior.

Years ago, Christ was just somebody that I read about in a book, or a concept that I talked about. But now he's a friend, and the only goal I have in my life is to be one with him.

That's something I never really thought about that deeply until these past few years. But now the one thing I encourage people to be is one with the Lord. Be one with Jesus in everything. He's alive and he loves you. That's it. That's everything. The whole purpose of our life is that we may all be one in him.

"When I heard people talking about God as a real person, I couldn't relate to that at all. If he was there to me, it was a conceptual thing."

Helen Bradley

Age 29, homemaker, married 6 years

MY STORY IS not a dramatic one. I wasn't down in the depths, and God didn't come to me in a single, explosive event. I never openly rebelled against God; I just hit a point in life where he wasn't especially close. It was as if I didn't want to be bothered. I always related to life primarily through my head rather than my heart, so God seemed more like a concept than a person to me. When I would hear people talking about God as a real person, I couldn't relate to that at all. My God didn't have much to do with my everyday, personal life. If he was there to me, it was a conceptual thing. He did run the universe in some kind of vague, detached way and was probably watching over us from a distance; but that was all.

God seemed so vague, in fact, and so far removed from me that even when I did pray, it was never with a conviction that he cared about answering me. I'd even ask other people to pray for me, because I was really sure that God wouldn't bother listening to me.

That approach to life was reflected in all my relationships, I suppose. I was pretty detached and self-contained. I liked an orderly life. I planned it day by day, and I didn't appreciate other people interfering. I was task-oriented rather than people-oriented. If I were to achieve a particular task, then my day would seem worthwhile.

Not surprisingly, I was also afraid of taking risks. That's one reason I had trouble with relationships; life seemed safer if I didn't get involved. I also hated making decisions about anything. I'd take ten steps down the road, then have to analyze everything to the nth degree. Even though I hated being so analytical, I was always weighing pros and cons, every aspect of every decision, so I was afraid to take any risks at all.

When I met my husband Tom, he began to help me, but in a very gentle way. He had always been withdrawn, but now he wanted to begin reaching out. He wanted a relationship. And so, very gently, he began opening me up to the possibility that my life could, and should, include more contact with people rather than simply with projects.

Then, when God knew we were ready, he dealt with our lives. But he, too, did things very gently. Even the way he brought us to our first prayer meeting was just a gentle nudge. It wasn't a big, dramatic thing, just a gentle notion that we should go. So one night we did. After that we kept returning. We made the Life in the Spirit Seminar and were baptized in the Holy Spirit, and again nothing par-

ticularly dramatic seemed to happen. It was a very
quiet, very gentle experience.

In a way, I guess I was even a little disappointed.
I'd almost expected more. But a week after we
were baptized in the Spirit, Tom and I went on
vacation, and it was then that I noticed the first
significant change in my life. To my surprise I began reading the Bible regularly, and liking it. That
was unusual for me. I also found myself able to face
some of my own shortcomings. For no particular
reason I'd begin to think of some area of my life
and decide: "I really have to do something about
this." Sometimes it even had me down, but it kept
happening; all of a sudden I'd notice things about
myself that needed to change.

Also, I began to have a whole new knowledge of
God. Again, it was very gentle, but it was so important to me. It was such a gift! I became convinced,
shortly after the seminar, that the "God of condemna-
tion" that I had been raised to believe in was not
really what God was all about. He was a God of love.
No matter what happened, he loved us. He always
had loved us. He always will love us. I really became
convinced of that. I still didn't have much of a personal relationship with him, even at that point, but I
knew positively that he was a God of love. And I clung
to that knowledge. I was so happy that God had
showed me that!

Tom and I soon joined a nearby prayer community
where we kept hearing about the importance of having a "personal relationship with Jesus." I began to
understand that this was something I didn't yet have.
I realized, though, that I was very close to having it,

because I had come to know God's love as a reality in my life.

Then one weekend it happened. I knew that there were many past experiences in my life that had hurt me badly, so I began to talk to the Lord about these. And deep in my heart, I listened to him respond. For the first time in my life, I was having a conversation with the Lord. I wasn't simply asking him for something; we had a real two-way conversation.

The conversation was so real that after we finished talking I even imagined that the Lord got up and started to leave, when I suddenly remembered a bad experience at a doctor's office. So I said "Wait a minute, I've got to tell you about the doctor's." And he answered, "Oh, I know about the doctor's. I was there. You talked to me then, and I heard you." It really hit me then: when we talk to him he responds. I thought, "Well, of course!"

It was suddenly so natural and real to experience God's love in this way. And this is the way I see Jesus now. He's a very loving, listening person who knows me and accepts me and loves me, and I love him.

Meditation

Jesus Is Saving

Jesus: noun derived from Hebrew Yeshua, a variation of Yehoshua, meaning "God is saving."

The name "Jesus" means "God is saving." His very presence in any given situation means "God is saving." Whenever he speaks, acts, or becomes part of our lives in any way, "God is saving."

We all need to be saved. Sometimes this need is more obvious to one person than to another. Sometimes, too, the fact that Jesus has acted to save someone is more apparent in one situation than another. But regardless of the circumstances, the purpose and meaning of the presence of Jesus is always the same—"God is saving."

"My brother had become a heroin addict. I didn't know what to do, but I wanted so badly to help him. I told the Lord that if he would really do something for my brother, then I would go to a prayer meeting."

Joan Wyss

Age 43, homemaker,
married 23 years, 4 children

WHEN JIM AND I were first married I prayed often, and God would answer me. Those were happy days. For the first time in my life, I began to find God through the words of the Bible. I really began to know him and would sing songs and pray to him as a natural part of my life.

But somewhere during those first years, between giving birth to four children, watching Jim become more involved in his job, and finding that life had been getting busier and busier, I began to feel more alone. I actually became afraid of people, until this fear grew so much that it became a monster in my life.

During this time I stopped reading the Bible. I hardly ever prayed anymore. I seemed so busy with the kids and everything. My days went by so fast that I never thought about God. After a while, when I tried to reach out to people, I'd find myself paralyzed with fear. The more I tried, the worse it got. Whenever I forced myself to go to coffee klatches in the neighborhood, I ended up worse. At Jim's company parties I would hang on to him for dear life; I was so terrified of people. A trip to the shopping center would make me cry—all the people there, I'd be so frightened. Or Jim would take me to the movies, and I'd walk into the back of the theater and see all the people and be frightened to death. We'd have to sit in the back, and I'd be torn with anxiety through the whole movie. It was really hard for me, and for him.

That was one trial. The second hit us at the same time and involved my younger brother David.

I was always very close to David. When he was just a baby I'd take turns with Mom rocking him at night. For his birthday I'd help buy baby clothes for him. He was very special. Our family never showed much emotion when I was growing up; we didn't hug or demonstrate our love. But when David came into the house, he brought out that show of love from everyone. A baby really brings out love, and that's what David had always meant to me. He came into my life as a source of love.

Now, at the same time that I had begun to feel so alone and afraid of people, David came to stay with us for a few days. He was just a teenager, but he had become a heroin addict.

I was crushed for him. When he was in the ninth grade he had been an A-student, president of his class. He was on the student council, an outstanding athlete, who had everything in the world going for him. He seemed so happy at the time. Then he got hurt playing football, and wasn't able to play any sports. He became disillusioned by the people he had thought were his friends—people in the school, in the student government. I think he was disillusioned with himself, too. So he started going around with kids who were involved with drugs and gradually got into them himself. Before long he had become a heroin addict. I didn't know what to do, but I wanted so badly to help him.

Finally he overdosed and ended up in the hospital. I went to see him and told him everything I could think of. I told him how much we loved him, that life was hard, but that if he really tried, he could make it. I told him about how Jim had worked hard and succeeded. If only David would do this, he would find happiness too. But nothing I could tell him could meet the needs that he had. I didn't know how deep his needs were. I couldn't see them or fill them.

When he finally got out of the hospital, I invited him to visit again, but he gave excuses. He wouldn't come. We sent him to a rehabilitation center, but it didn't help. The first thing they did was shave his head. Next they put him in a very hard-core group that he didn't feel a part of. Before long he ran away from the center.

A psychologist started to work with him, who was really a kind man. He tried so hard to help. He would even drive out in the middle of the night to sit with David and drive him around. But he couldn't help either.

Then we tried methadone. David went to a clinic

and before long was hooked on methadone. He'd come to see me, and he'd scratch and scratch and sleep on the couch half the day, and he had such a darkness in his eyes. It was a look that really scared me, because it was a death look. He told me that he had overdosed before. The last time, he had prayed repeatedly, "Please God, don't let it be this time." He knew, you see. He knew that he was somehow in death. But he also knew that God was there. Down deep he believed, but he was resisting God.

He claimed he was an atheist, but when he got to that point of death, he would reach out to God. In fact, one time when he overdosed his heart actually stopped beating, and he cried out in his mind, "Oh God, if you're there, please save me," and his heart started beating again. But he still didn't accept God.

About the same time, my sister started going to weekly prayer meetings, and she would talk to me about prayer and the Lord. I resisted going to the meetings because of my fear of people, but I knew that there was also great despair in my heart. I was calling out so hard to God, but I didn't hear any answer. So I prayed secretly, in my own heart, and I told the Lord that if he would really do something for my brother, then I would go to a prayer meeting.

Well, the Lord did. I wouldn't go to a meeting at that point, but my sister took David to one. He just listened that first night, and left without making any commitment, but the next week he went back on his own. Then, after the prayer meeting was over, he went up to be prayed with. The people layed their hands on him and prayed, and he just reached out his arms and said, "Jesus Christ, if you really are the Son of God, please save me." And Jesus saved him. Jesus Christ healed David totally of that long addiction, on the spot. He even healed him of the methadone addiction. He healed him instantly and completely. There was no withdrawal. The death-look went out of his eyes and he was totally free, completely healed. The next time I saw him I looked into his eyes and saw life.

The clinic even called to ask why he didn't come in for his next methadone appointment, and he told them that Jesus saved him. They didn't believe him, but it was true. That was seven years ago, and he's never had to go back to drugs. We continually saw the light in his eyes after that, and from that time on it was pure joy to be around him. It was like watching a small child walk again. He was so in love with Jesus. It was like heaven itself to be near him. He said it was as though God had wrapped him in a big blanket and put him in a feather bed, and that he just felt God's love constantly. It was a beautiful experience.

After I saw that, of course, I wanted what he had. I needed it. I had seen the miracle, and now I needed a miracle, because I was still very afraid of people. I had also promised the Lord that I'd go to a prayer meeting, so I did go, though I was still very much afraid. And the Lord touched me there. He blessed me with his presence and he began to change me.

I went to a Life in the Spirit Seminar and was prayed with to be baptized in the Holy Spirit. I really expected the same kind of extraordinary experience that David had, and was somewhat disillusioned when I didn't receive it. But the night I was prayed for, I told the people that I felt I had become part of a family. And I know now that God gave me a loving family of people, so I wouldn't have to be afraid, a family I could go to for love and support.

I was even asked if I would take part in the introductory session before the prayer meetings, where new people are greeted. I was terrified to be asked to meet new people every week, but I said, "Yes." I felt that the Lord was asking me to do this. So from then on, week after week, I would proclaim the good news about Jesus Christ, especially as I had seen it in David's life. And it was in proclaiming this that I was healed and set free. I became very comfortable with people and loved to be with them again.

The more I spoke about Jesus, the freer I became. At first it seemed like the hardest thing in the world to do. But it was God's healing plan for my life.

After that, my faith in God grew steadily. I believed that he wanted to work a miracle in my whole family. My relationship with Jim was not as good as it should have been at that time. The world just seemed to be pulling at us. Jim's work kept demanding more of him at the same time I had been leaning on him for everything. He just couldn't take the pressure. The more I demanded, the more he ran. But now I felt so much trust in God! I was sure that God had a plan for our lives, and that he was working constantly to draw us into that plan. Over the next year I saw again how true the Lord is to his word. Our daughter recommitted her life to the Lord. Then Jim began to share in our prayers and all that God was doing in our lives. All of our children, one by one, took Jesus into their lives in a new and real way.

Life has not always been easy since I've entered

into a more personal relationship with Christ, but I can really see that new strength is growing in me. He's not just a surface-working God to me anymore. I can remember asking God in the past to make me a stronger person, someone with deeper faith, and he's done that. I know now that I couldn't have found the Lord the way I have if I hadn't experienced some of the valleys I've been in. Maybe some people could, but I couldn't. He is a miracle-working God, and I love him!

"I didn't want anything to do with prayer meetings. My reluctance, I think, stemmed in large part from an unwillingness to listen to someone else, especially when that 'someone else' was my wife and my children."

Jim Wyss

Age 46, president of a tool and die company, married 23 years, 4 children

I CAME FROM a family with a very domineering father. He knew how to play with us when we were children, but he never instilled in us a belief that we really amounted to much. I remember that the neighboring farmer was the first man to ever compliment me, to tell me that I did a good job at something.

As a result, I was determined to prove myself, to make good on my own. During the first years of my marriage I thought of myself as a self-made man, a guy really making sure that my life was going to amount to something, that my family was going to be well taken care of. I thought there wasn't anything, no matter how bad it was, that I couldn't somehow work through. Of course, my constant striving for success really robbed Joan and the rest of my family of my time and attention.

Eight or nine years ago, I started to go to Mass every day. I knew God then as someone to run to when I was in trouble. I also knew him as a God who kept close track of things. I thought I could make up for some of the things I had done, so going to Mass in the mornings was important to me. And God certainly worked through my experience of the Mass. I know he used it to bring me to where I am today.

After my wife's brother was healed miraculously of heroin addiction, she became very involved with Jesus through prayer meetings at our church and was really able to make a new and deeper commitment to God. Our oldest daughter Christie was also recommitting her life to God, but I didn't want anything to do with their prayer meetings. We even had several disagreements about why I refused to take some part in what they were doing.

My reluctance, I think, stemmed from my unwillingness to listen to someone else, especially when that "someone else" was my wife and children. One night, Joan mentioned that there was going to be a Mass incorporated into the prayer meeting, and that's what the Lord used to draw me closer to him. I was really attached to the Mass, so I agreed to go with her that one evening.

What I experienced at Mass on that first evening was a deep peace within myself. Though I didn't know what it was at the time, I realized something was happening that was different from anything I had experienced before.

As a result of the peace I felt that night, I joined

Joan at one of the prayer meetings within the next week or two. I don't think I've missed one since, except when I happened to be out-of-town. Since then, God has really begun to work new and wonderful things in my life, to change me as a person.

He hasn't so much changed the circumstances around me. But he has changed me. Much to my surprise, he began by using Joan and the children to lead me closer to himself. Who would have figured that? As the man of the house, I had always thought that I had to be the one to lead the family, no matter where we were going—down the block or all the way to heaven. But God showed me through Joan and the children how much he could really love me if I'd only let him.

Over the past few years, he's changed the way I look at life. He took away a lot of that hard-driven need for success the way the world measures it. Yet, at the same time, he's allowed me to achieve things without so much effort on my own part. I'm depending on him now in everything.

He's also taught me how to listen. I can see and hear what's hurting someone else now, and what I've done to hurt them. And he's given me the ability to say, "I'm sorry." It's terrible to look back and realize that there were many years when I couldn't do that. I never told anyone I was sorry, not even Joan or the kids. Now I can say it and mean it. Our family has a much fuller relationship than either Joan or I once thought possible. And we continue to become closer every day.

I'll always remember, not long ago, sitting on the swing in the backyard with Joan. She looked me in the eye and said, "We're making it, aren't we, Jim?" After twenty-three years of marriage we shouldn't have to say that to each other, but I think it's just great that God brought us to a point where we can say it. We no longer take each other for granted, and we know how much Christ loves us.

That's the good news: that Christ first loved us. He is a very different God than I ever imagined. He's a God that really loves me. He loves Joan and every one of our children. He loves every person who comes into our lives, and he continues to show his love to us every day.

*"All my struggling to make myself
happy had led me to that point. I had
lost my marriage, my job, my house,
and my car. I was fifteen-thousand
dollars in debt, and I even lost what
little peace of mind I once had."*

Gregg Weddle

Age 30, computer programmer analyst,
married 2 years, 2 children

BEFORE I CAME to know Jesus Christ, my life was
really a search for happiness, though I was striving
after things that didn't have happiness in them:
money, sex, jobs, possessions, psychic power, and
other things.

Eventually, it all started to fall apart. My marriage
collapsed after just two years. My job was shaky, and
my whole life threatened to come apart. I wasn't
happy, and I was really feeling desperate.

One night, on the way home from an astrology
class, everything collapsed. I was driving my new
Jaguar, with my boss' secretary in the seat beside me,
when I ran into another car head-on. She was cut up
very badly and the couple in the other car, who were

in their seventies, were seriously injured. I totaled my car, but since I had no insurance, I couldn't replace it. I lost my job due to the bad feelings the accident caused. After that I had to give up my house, because I couldn't make the payments. Worst of all, a few weeks later, the man injured in the other car died. Though his death couldn't legally be blamed on the accident, in my heart I've always wondered.

So all my struggling to make myself happy had led me to that point. I had lost my marriage, my job, my house, and my car. I was fifteen-thousand dollars in debt because of all the medical bills, and I even lost what little peace of mind I once had, because of the man who died after the accident. It was as if the whole world had ended. There was nothing but darkness. It culminated on Thanksgiving Day. I was totally alone, in a little one-room apartment—no job, no transportation, no friends. I went to a restaurant, bought a carry-out Thanksgiving dinner, and took it back to my apartment. In the silence, without anything or anyone to give thanks for, I ate my dinner. It was so terrible. I was so alone.

After that experience I was determined to find meaning in something, so I decided to become more deeply involved in the occult. If material power couldn't make me happy, then maybe spiritual power would. I began taking yoga classes and attended various occult workshops. In fact, I was very quickly accepted into the state's major occult society, a broad-based metaphysical society that forms an umbrella over all the occult activities in the state. It includes various branches of astrology, psychic healing, fortune-telling, seances, witchcraft, even Satanism. I was accepted, not just by a branch, but by the society's leaders. As strange as it may sound, they told me I was a special being that had been sent to earth, someone sent from another world, another dimension. I had been sent to earth, they said, to tell everybody the truth. And the more I became involved in occult practices, the more spiritual power I actually began to experience.

I experienced mind-control over other people, as well as control and direction within myself. For example, one time I was supposed to go to a meeting in Toledo, the society's headquarters for the Midwest. I had only passed through Toledo twice before, so I didn't know the city and didn't know how to get to the meeting. But I decided I didn't need a map. Instead, I would let my psychic power guide me. So I drove to Toledo, and when I arrived, I literally followed my spirit guide: "Turn left here, turn right there," and so on. I was turning right and left until I pulled up and stopped in front of a house. I walked up and rang the bell, and that was it. The meeting I was looking for was in that house.

I can only tell you two things about the inner voice that directed me. First, it was real. It was telling me exactly when and where to turn and when to stop. Second, it wasn't anything holy speaking to me. It was harsh, somehow; it wasn't God, but it was real. Psychic and spirit power in the occult are real. There is power, but it doesn't come from God.

By this time I was deeply involved, a "special being" who experienced extraordinary psychic realities. At the same time, my sister in Milwaukee, who was a Christian, grew very concerned about me. She sent me a book about the spiritual warfare going on today between Christ and Satan. Well, I wasn't interested in Christianity at that time, so I threw the book in the corner as soon as I received it. But God had other ways to reach me.

One night I attended a vegetarian dinner where I happened to meet a Christian pastor. The next week, he sent me a Bible. I was preparing to attend an occult convention that same weekend, so it occured to me to take that Bible along. Many people in the occult admit there's wisdom in the Bible; you just have to interpret it their way. So I took it, and began to read it over the weekend. The more I read, the less peaceful I felt about my life. In fact, I spent the whole weekend feeling very unpeaceful.

Finally, after a week of this, I decided to read the book that my sister had sent about spiritual warfare. I couldn't put it down. It described everything I had seen and experienced in the occult—all the powers and some of the miracles—only it showed that they didn't really come from God, but were from Satan. Their purpose was not to heal and make happy, but to draw people farther away from God, from the healing and happiness that would last forever. I knew without the slightest doubt that what the book was describing had happened to me. I realized that I didn't know God in the least and was very far from possessing his peace. When I realized that I had been listening to Satan, I was horrified.

I wanted to pray, but didn't know how. The only thing I had to help me was a family heirloom, a rosary that belonged to my grandmother. I hadn't wanted to throw away something she treasured. So I rushed through my things and found the rosary. Then I got down on my knees and prayed. I prayed with such a deep need, asking Mary to pray for me, asking God to help me, somehow.

As I prayed I experienced physical manifestations of being freed from the power that Satan had used in my life. I was in my dark basement apartment. It was late at night, but as I called out to God in prayer there were very bright flashes of light in that room, and as I prayed I felt freer and more peaceful and happy.

At the end of that rosary, I wanted to go to Confession, so I drove to a church and sat in front of it until six-thirty in the morning, when it opened. Then I asked for the priest. I poured out everything, all the selfishness, the things I had done, the hurt I had caused, all the things I had tried to take for myself. When he finished praying with me, I felt totally free. It was beautiful! I went to Mass and Communion, and I felt so great. I drove home singing and thanking God all the way. I had such a sense that he loved me, and that he had rescued me.

My whole life has changed since then. I moved back in with my folks, where the Lord accomplished a lot of healing. He really showed me how to love them. I found jobs and began to pay off the debts I had. Scripture came alive for me, and I spent a lot of time in prayer. And God even led me to a new family, a prayer community.

I was amazed at the first prayer meeting I went to—at all the people who were praising God, and who were excited about him. Once I found them, I kept coming back. I even found that there was cause for having my first marriage annulled, and now the

Lord has given me a new wife and family.

So I can't thank God enough, for saving me, loving me, giving me the happiness I was trying so hard to find. I'm not looking desperately for love anymore. I've got it. I don't have to fight for anything now. I know I can trust him. Times can still be hard, but Jesus really is a loving person. Even when I'm stubborn, he just allows me to see how that always turns against me, and I remember that I can't be happy that way.

Now Jesus is my Lord. Sometimes it's as though he's not just talking to me; he's singing. There's so much joy in him. He's the Lord of everything, but he's also childlike in a way; he's so joyful.

He knows what it means to be a child, and now he invites me to live as a child of God.

"For twenty-five years I had lived in alcoholism. But I had never prayed for myself. So at that time I got down on my knees, and I just said, 'Lord, you've got to help me.'"

Ron Edwards

Age 45, scheduler for a manufacturing corporation, married 22 years, 6 children

I GUESS I was typical in a lot of ways. I was raised as a Catholic and went to Catholic schools, and was baptized and confirmed. But I realize now that somehow I never really knew God very well. In fact, I only called for him when I was really in trouble. I figured I could rely on him at those times and then put him away until I needed him again. To me, Jesus was someone I had learned about but didn't really know.

By the time I was eighteen, I was drinking, and for the next twenty-five years I drank heavily. I was an alcoholic. Even so, I always thought I was in control of my drinking. But the more control I thought I had, the more out of control I really was. For twenty-five years I lived in alcoholism, but it wasn't until the day

I was going to lose my job because of my drinking problem that I admitted I was really an alcoholic, in terrible trouble.

That really shook me. My wife had been praying for me for a long time, but I had never prayed for myself. So at that time I got down on my knees, and I just said, "Lord, you've got to help me." It was that simple. And, while I had no idea at the time, I know now that I was healed right then of twenty-five years of alcoholism.

For anyone familiar with alcoholism, that may seem pretty hard to believe. But it's the truth. God did that for me, and I didn't even know it at the time. But after two weeks the situation at work had settled down, and I hadn't had even one drink. By then I figured something was really up. I still wasn't sure that God had done anything, but I was discovering that my desire to drink had left me. I realized after those first two weeks that alcohol was the last thing on my mind. And then, when I actually smelled it, it didn't have the same effect. In fact, it made me nauseous. After twenty-five years, I was finally free of it.

That was four years ago, and I haven't touched alcohol since. I've had no desire for it. I even receive Communion under both forms, and it has no bad effects, nothing to do with alcoholism at all. And the most amazing thing to me is that I never experienced withdrawal.

When I realized what had happened, I thought: "Oh, Lord, why me? Why are you so good to me?" But before long, I knew that Jesus wanted to do even more.

For thirty years, I had been a chain-smoker at the rate of two packs a day. When I drank, I'd smoke three packs. Then one day, on my way to work, I began to think about my smoking. I decided to trust the Lord and said, "Lord, I'll put this in your hands, too. Let's see how long it will be before I smoke again." With that, I threw my cigarettes out. I haven't touched one since. It's been three years, and again, there was no withdrawal, no agony. I have no desire to smoke. It's like the alcohol. It just disappeared from my life.

For over twenty years I had a severe acne condition. Every month I had to go to the doctor because of it. Now it's gone. That was over three years ago, and it hasn't come back. All of these things are signs to me of the way Christ has changed my whole life in just the last four years.

Before I was cured of alcoholism, my wife has asked me to attend a prayer meeting with her. But I'm the kind of person that needs a lot of proof before I get into something. I just don't accept things at face value. So Betty had been going by herself for awhile. When she'd go I'd say, "Pray for me," but when she'd come back I'd ridicule her. I'd put her down for talking about Jesus. She'd tell me what happened at the prayer meeting, and I'd say, "That's fine for those people, but not for me."

Finally, after a year-and-a-half, back when I was still drinking, I went to a meeting with her, and frankly I wasn't all that knocked out about it. In fact, it turned me off. I thought, "Hey, all these people should get themselves locked up or something." It was unreal to me, to see people praising God the way they did. But I did return a second time. There was something about it that made me go back.

I guess what got me was the sincerity. These people were praying in ways that I was uncomfortable with at the time, but they were obviously sincere. It wasn't a plastic meeting; it wasn't faked. I figured that if it was just man-made, it would have to have been faked. But it wasn't. So after that, I dropped in every few weeks.

I guess a lot of people were praying for me during those months. And finally, like I said, I prayed for something to happen myself, and it did. I don't think I even believed myself that anything would change when I prayed. But the Lord worked. Maybe it was everyone else's prayers. Maybe it was because my faith was so weak that God figured I needed to see something special. Whatever the reason, he showed me that he's real. He changed my whole life—my relationship with my wife and kids, the way I feel about myself, the way I perform my job. Everything in my life has changed for the better.

I go to prayer meetings now and love them. I thank God, because he's real to me. The healings I experienced weren't just freak things. They were gifts from a person, a real person. Jesus wanted me to understand that, and I do.

Today, I know that Jesus is my brother. He's somebody I can really talk to. Anytime I want to discuss something, I can go to him on a one-to-one basis. He knows me, and I know him.

That's why I can tell people today, "When Jesus went to the cross, he had you in mind. He knows your problems, and he knows you by name." I can say that to people, because now I know it's true.

*"I was really in the pits. We had six
children; my husband was an alcoholic;
and I was feeling unloved and
unappreciated right inside my own
home."*

Betty Edwards

Age 42, homemaker,
married 22 years, 6 children

SEVEN YEARS AGO I was really in the pits. We had
six children; my husband was an alcoholic; and I was
feeling unloved and unappreciated right inside my
own home. I went through life like the song says:
laughing on the outside, crying on the inside. But
pain always comes out in some way. It makes itself
felt.

My family was arguing and fighting and hating one
another constantly. I'd talk to friends, and they'd say,
"Oh, that's normal. Everybody does that." But I knew
in my heart that it wasn't the way it was meant to be.
Everybody couldn't do that. God couldn't really in-
tend families to live like that.

Even at that time, God really was a deep part of my
life. Though I didn't pray every day, or believe that

God could or would change everything that was wrong in my life, I did believe in him. In fact, I spent a lot of time thanking God for all he had given me, in spite of the problems. But even so, I experienced such an emptiness about where I was and what I was doing. So much was missing, and I was terribly lonely.

Then one summer I volunteered to help with a high school religion program, and that's how God reached me in a new way. I wanted to give something to him, and he turned around and gave me a whole new life.

One night one of the other teachers invited me to go with him and several others to a prayer meeting at a nearby college. When we went, I was awe-struck. Everyone was praising God. It was super. It was different than what I was used to, but I believed that if people were praising God, then something good was going on.

A few weeks later, I decided to go to a prayer meeting at a neighboring parish, and I've been thanking God ever since. My whole life has changed: my home, my attitudes, my relationship with Ron and the kids, even Ron's alcoholism.

The biggest change, though, and the reason for all the others, is my new relationship with Jesus. I knew a lot about Jesus before, but I never knew him very personally, the way he wants us to know him. I grew up with a "This is your cross, bear it" attitude. In fact, I attended those first few prayer meetings not so much because I wanted to know Jesus, but because I wanted to join something, anything. I always felt more appreciated outside my home than inside.

Now, though, it's easy for me to love, talk with, and

trust the Lord, because I know he loves me. I'm loved by my family and by him. He's so good. He's just walked through our home healing and saving and passing out miracles left and right—to Ron and me, the kids, our friends, prayer community, and parish. I've seen so many mountains moved, so much joy and love given to people.

That's what Jesus is: he's love. And his love makes all the difference in the world.

"I spent most of my life convinced that there was nothing about me that people could really love. Finally, about four years ago, I started to break apart. I came totally undone, and it scared me to death."

Ray Maloney

Age 52, headmaster of a private academy, married 21 years, 3 children (one deceased)

FOR MOST OF my life I believed that I wasn't of any importance to anyone. That puzzles people when I say this, because I've always seemed successful. But I spent most of my life convinced that there was nothing about me that people could really love. As a result, I could never really love others.

My memory of these feelings of rejection go back to when I was a young child. My mother died when I was four, and her death seemed like a rejection to me. I told myself, "She's left me. She doesn't want to be with me."

I also grew up with a father who was incapable of showing genuine love. As a result, I never had much of a relationship with him. In fact, the only feelings I

ever had toward my father were ones of hatred and
fear.

To deal with all this, I had constructed a front, a
mask to cover my insecurity. I wasn't really confident,
I was just a good actor. I can remember many times in
class, for example, when I was putting on a presenta-
tion, saying to myself, "I'm pulling it off again." I
knew that I didn't look scared. I was hiding it, getting
away with it one more time, not showing anyone how
much I hurt.

Finally, about four years ago, as happens sooner or
later to everyone under that kind of strain, I started to
break apart. It's possible to struggle with intense
feelings of fear and anxiety for only so long. I began to
realize that I couldn't pull it off any more. I couldn't
go back to school pretending everything was going
great when inside I knew I was falling apart.

It happened when I was in Chicago on a trip to visit
schools. I came suddenly and totally unglued. My
personality seemed to disintegrate. I just sat and
cried. I couldn't even talk. I came totally undone, and
it scared me to death. I knew it was happening, but I
didn't know how to handle it.

When I got home, I told my wife everything. She
had no idea what was inside of me, I had hidden it so
well. But I told her the whole story, beginning to
end, and we decided that I needed professional help.

I went into therapy immediately. I was lucky, since
I knew the psychologist and trusted him. And he
showed me a lot about my mother and father, my
feelings of rejection, anger, and so on.

I also realized during this time that my feelings
about my father were tied into my feelings about

God. As a result, my relationship with God was distant and fearful. I thought, "If I do anything at all with God, I'll just displease him, so I better not get involved." It was the same thing that I had decided about my relationship with my father. It seemed better to do nothing than suffer another rejection. Of course that meant there was no real relationship at all.

About that time, a young man from a prayer community in Ann Arbor stopped into school selling magazine advertising space. In the course of our conversation he spoke very freely about Jesus. I wasn't all that interested, frankly, but something about this man clicked with me. I believed he did know God. So within a month, I wrote him a letter saying I'd like to hear more, and I'd like some help in learning how to pray.

It was unusual for me to write a letter like that to someone I had just met, but the young man, whose name was Pete, did write back. He gave me some suggestions, which I never did follow, and then we lost contact.

It seemed a fairly minor incident, a reaching out of some kind, but nothing really significant came of it at the time.

Meanwhile, my therapy continued, but I didn't experience any healing. Months went by. Even though I had begun to understand the things that had hurt me and caused my anger, I didn't seem to be getting any better. I was still angry, still hurt, still a wreck.

Then one night I came apart again. For an entire week I couldn't stop crying. I didn't know what to do, and even considered suicide. I was dissolving. It was all so totally destructive. The world seemed to be falling apart, and it was falling on me.

My therapist told me that this time I would have to handle things on my own, which meant that if I was going to keep everyone from discovering what had happened, I'd have to pull myself together enough to get back to school.

I did, somehow. But I knew now that everything was temporary. I was doomed; I saw no hope. But I did go to school. And on that day, when I walked into school, Jesus met me and changed everything.

I walked into my office and Pete was there, back again. I was really surprised, because he hadn't called, written, or anything.

He said, "I'm not sure why I'm here. I was going to lunch in another area, but I suddenly felt that I should come and see you."

I told him that I really needed help, very badly, and he just said, "I love you, and Jesus loves you, too." Then he said he'd like to pray for me.

I wasn't even sure what that meant, but I sat down, right there in my office. Pete held one of my hands and put his other hand on my head. Then he prayed that the Father would deliver me from all that was hurting me. He didn't even know what was bothering me. He just prayed that the Father would deliver me. And as soon as he prayed that simple prayer, I could feel all of this hurt and anger and fear starting to drain out of me. There was no crying, nothing emotional about it. Pete also prayed in tongues. Then he praised the Father for creating me. Through the whole prayer, I could physically feel anger, pain, and hatred draining out of me. In its place was a sensation of warmth and peace.

The whole thing was over in five minutes. That's all it took. The depression I had lived with and struggled with for so many years was gone, and it hasn't returned. That was over three years ago. God healed me on that day.

Since then, God has changed me in so many ways. There are still struggles in my life, some very difficult, but I know I'm growing. He's given me so many brothers and sisters, and he's given me a very real, constant knowledge that I am loved. I can really accept love now, and I'm able to love other people. In my relationship with my wife and kids, with people at school, with everyone, I can express my love now, and I can accept theirs.

As a result of all this healing, I have a very certain sense of how real Jesus is. I never used to be quite that sure about it. Now I just want to say, "Hey, look everybody! He's really alive!"

I gave him my life when it was all in pieces, and he gave it back and it was healed. Not only that, but he gave me a strong gift of love to keep it healed.

That's what I was missing all these years. It's what so many people are missing. But it's there for the asking. Because Jesus really is alive.

Meditation

A Personal Relationship with Jesus

"You search the scriptures, for you believe they give you eternal life. And the scriptures point to me! Yet you won't come to me that I can give you this life eternal" (Jn 5:39-40).

This passage points to the central discovery made by each of the people in this book, and by Christians everywhere: knowing about Jesus Christ doesn't make us whole, happy, or sanctified. Knowing about Jesus doesn't even make us Christian. We're invited to know Jesus personally, and through that personal relationship to receive the love God offers us.

There's a tremendous difference between knowing about Christ and knowing Christ personally. On the one hand are those who know Christianity simply as a standard of morality, a way of life, an ethical system, or an intellectual position. On the other hand are those who actually know Jesus Christ. They have more than a set of principles; they have a personal relationship with the man Jesus.

Without this personal relationship, you have the lifeless situation that Jesus grieves over in the passage quoted above. With it you have, again and again, experiences like those shared throughout this book.

"God always seemed fairly distant from us. He was King, and we were down here. He was real and cared for us, but we couldn't get too close to him."

Frank Petri

Age 71, married 45 years, 6 children (one deceased)

SEVEN YEARS AGO our forty-year marriage was under a great deal of stress. My health wasn't good, and I was so nervous about everything that I would stay awake half the night worrying. My spiritual life was strained. It wasn't joyful or peaceful and neither was I.

Today, my entire life has been changed. I've never been happier than I am now.

My new life began when our pastor mentioned in one of his homilies that he might be starting a prayer meeting in our parish. After Mass I asked him to let me know if he did. I had read a little about the new prayer movement, and what I had read interested me. I was skeptical, but interested.

Three weeks later, our pastor came up to me and said, "We're having a meeting tomorrow night. Come and join us." I was surprised that he had moved so quickly, but my wife Ernestine and I went.

It was just a small meeting, four or five people, but that was the beginning. We didn't immediately feel at home there, either. We both thought that maybe it was too far out for us. In fact, when we left that first meeting, we really weren't interested in returning.

We were raised in a very conservative era, and God always seemed fairly distant from us. He was King, and we were down here. He was real and cared for us, but we couldn't get too close to him. We just weren't raised with the expectation that we could know God personally. Our training said that you didn't talk in church. You didn't really express closeness with even your own brothers and sisters, so we didn't hug other people or show our emotions very much. Our culture was against it, so we weren't really at home with the attitude of the prayer meeting. To see people praying in tongues, praising God out loud, talking to him personally, raising their hands in prayer, and hugging one another was really foreign to us.

But something drew us back. When the next week rolled around, we said, "Let's try it just once more." And when we went back, we realized why we had returned. It was the faith of the young people there, with their sharings and obvious dedication to God. It just impressed us no end.

I said to my wife, "There must be something good here. Young people, any people, don't do all this unless something good is happening." So we kept going back. And every time we went, we seemed to draw closer to Jesus.

I was finally prayed with to be baptized in the Holy

Spirit, but I was honestly disappointed. I had come to expect a lot, but I didn't feel anything. I knew that for some people it had been a tremendous experience, but it seemed as though nothing had happened to me.

A week later, in the middle of the night, I woke up crying like a baby and couldn't stop. It just poured out of me. I was really alarmed. I woke up Ernestine and said to her, "What's wrong with me? I've never done this before in my life! Something's wrong, I can't stop crying!" She said, "The Holy Spirit is touching you. I'm sure of it." And she prayed for me, and I prayed. On that night, I felt a release of all this tension, of deep hurts from the past. All the pain I had experienced in our relationship as husband and wife, as well as hurts from my whole life, came back to me, and I was freed. I had been holding everything inside, and I couldn't forgive. So often, I thought that I was right and the other person was wrong. Now I realized that I had a hostility in me, all this sin in me, and that I was being set free. God just took it all away. It was extraordinary and beautiful.

From that night on there has been a total change in my life. Not all the changes have been abrupt, but they all stemmed from that night.

I am so much happier now. God doesn't seem like a dictator to me anymore. He's a loving father, and Jesus is a wonderful brother who I can share all my troubles with. He loves me and really helps me. I used to be afraid to turn to God. It meant I had to go before the King, and I'd have to be in just the right mood. Now, no matter what, I can go to my Father. I can go to my Brother. I can ask him to forgive me and he does. Before, when I tried to pray, worries and anxieties would rush into my mind. Now I can leave them to Jesus.

God has changed me physically, spiritually, and emotionally. Today, at seventy-one years of age, I feel better than I did fifteen years ago.

My relationship with Ernestine is so much deeper. We used to love each other, but it wasn't a total, sharing love. I would never think of taking Ernestine's hand at the table and holding it, for instance. We just didn't relate that way. Now we hold hands a lot. We really love each other and aren't afraid to show it. We still have misunderstandings, but Jesus shows us how to work them out. At this point in our lives we have a better marriage than seven or seventeen or twenty-seven years ago. It seems incredible, but it's true.

Life used to be a terrific strain. Now, after all these years, it's a joy to be alive. God is so good.

"All through these years I always tried to do his will, but there was always something missing. No matter how hard I tried, life remained incomplete."

Ernestine Petri

Age 67, homemaker, married 45 years,
6 children (one deceased)

I WAS BORN in Austria. My mother was a governess; my father died when I was young. In 1916, we had to move to Hungary, where there was food, but in 1919, when they had a revolution, we left for England because my mother was English. Later we emigrated to Canada, where I met Frank. We were married during the Great Depression. Our first baby died, and the next year I had a tubular pregnancy and had to be operated on after only four months.

All through these turbulent years, I knew that God was there. I always tried to do his will, but there was always something missing. No matter how hard I tried, life remained incomplete.

Just seven years ago, our pastor talked about a new prayer meeting at church, and Frank and I were curious. I remember thinking, "That 'something' is still missing, so I might as well find out about this."

At that first meeting, though, I really questioned why I was there. We weren't at all used to praising God that openly. Yet, because of my sense of incompleteness, I still felt that the Lord might be leading me to the prayer meetings. So we continued to attend. Each week, something would draw us back, though I still felt uncomfortable. That's why I encourage people now to have patience. I tell them how hesitant I was at first.

Then one night, I knew why I was there. My whole relationship with God started to change. I began to understand what Jesus had done for me. For the first time ever, I understood what it meant that he took all of my sins into himself and destroyed their power to kill me. I knew that I had simply to accept that gift. I had never really understood what it meant that Jesus saved me. And now I really do.

Before, God seemed so far away. I loved and adored him and knew that he loved me. But I didn't experience the intimacy with God that I felt after I was baptized in the Holy Spirit.

Seven years ago, God still seemed far away. Now I know that God is right here within me.

That was the gap, you see. That was the "something" that was always missing—that intimate relationship, that real closeness that makes God my best friend and companion, as well as my God.

I've found what I was missing. It was in Jesus, all the time. I've experienced his closeness so powerfully at times that it overwhelms me. After sixty years, I can praise God and mean it, because the life I lead comes from a heart that's really full.

"Everything with me was rejection. I felt that nobody wanted me or approved of me. I couldn't live up to anything people expected of me."

Richard Letissier

Age 42, maintenance man

JESUS SAID TO forgive one another as he's forgiven us, but I've always found it hard to forgive people. When I was growing up I was hurt a lot, and the scars and embarrassments stayed with me. My whole upbringing was full of them.

I have a speech impediment, and that was the cause for a lot of it. It was such a burden and I felt so much guilt because of it.

As I grew up, my mother was close to me, but my dad was always too busy to give me the kind of love and support I needed, so I rebelled. I took out my anger and frustration on the school authorities.

A lot of my hurt had to do with my relationship with my brother. He had no impediments. In fact, he was way ahead of me in everything: in looks, intelligence, school, sports—everything. I tried to follow in his footsteps, so everyone would always compare us to one another. I suppose my parents did, too. So I grew up with this added resentment.

I was also left-handed, and again, it was pointed out to me that I was different. Society was made for other people. So everything with me was rejection. I'd look at society and my impediments. That was rejection. I looked for approval from my father. That was rejection. I was compared to my brother. That was rejection. As I progressed through school, I fell behind several grades. I became violent with the kids, the teachers, with everybody. I felt that nobody wanted me or approved of me. I couldn't live up to anything people expected of me. And I didn't know what I wanted out of life, what I wanted to be or what talents or abilities I had.

My mother died in 1963. Before she died, I remember her asking, "What are you going to do with your life?" I told her I didn't know. She said, "But you have to do something." All I could say in response was that I really had no idea what I was going to do. I was just so empty and confused, and I hated myself so much. When I looked at myself, all I saw was darkness. My image of myself was so bad that I couldn't communicate. I was too shy. I was afraid of failing again in anything.

During all of these years, I had no relationship with God, but I did have one discipline that stuck with me. I went to church on Sunday. It was something I could do, I guess. I wouldn't be rejected doing that. And I'm sure that's how the Lord saved me.

When I was thirty-five, my mother had been dead for a few years and my father had remarried and moved out, so I was totally alone and really unhappy.

The doctor had me taking tranquilizers three times a day, but that didn't help. They put me to sleep, but when I woke up my problems would still be there. Then one day in church the priest talked so beautifully about the love of God that it really touched me. It was the first time in my life I'd ever really been moved by that kind of thing. So I went to see him after Mass. Then I went back to talk with him again a few times, and he really became a good friend to me. He even used to take me out to the show sometimes. One night he said, "I've decided not to go to a movie tonight. I'm going to take you to a prayer meeting instead, if that's OK." Well, I was game. I didn't know what it was, but I said I'd go. He just told me that he thought it might help me in my search, so I went to my first prayer meeting.

When I got there I could see the love in peoples' eyes. I knew they accepted me for who I was. There was an affection going out from them to me, and this really touched me. So I kept going back.

About the third meeting, they prayed with me for the Baptism of the Holy Spirit. I wasn't sure what it was, but they asked if anybody wanted to be prayed with, and I said, "Sure." I'd be prayed with for anything. So they prayed with me.

Nothing happened that I could tell; there were no bells, no lights or anything, but they told me that the Lord was going to give me more peace in my life. And that's exactly what happened. In just the next few months, I got a lot closer to God, and I began to really experience a change. For the first time in my life I felt at peace. The most wonderful inner peace started coming into me. I couldn't explain it or describe it, but it was the first time in my life that I began to feel secure.

Then I read about forgiveness and about how Jesus lets us go back into our life and forgive people, and I wanted to do that. I would close my eyes and just let the Holy Spirit take over. I would remember the past and repeat peoples' names out loud, just saying them over and over again, asking the Lord to let his Spirit of forgiveness flow through me. And he did that. For the first time ever, I felt my burdens of guilt and resentment and anger lift from me, and I knew that the Lord was entering my life in a whole new way. I would feel a glow, like a peace, a grace, a love, from the top of my head to the bottom of my feet. I was being washed clean—physically, emotionally, and spiritually.

Every night I would pray, and I'd forgive, and I was so blessed. This was my beginning, the start of my new life. The old me was passing away, and now there was a new one. Finally, saving the best for last, God let me see that what he had given me was a really close friendship with Jesus.

My relationship with him today is one of real security. I'm secure in him. I am secure in his love, totally. No matter what comes, whatever trials, I know that he's with me. He's my companion, my brother and friend, and I know he won't fail me, no matter what.

He's healed my temper and my nerves. I don't need tranquilizers anymore. I used to have such trouble reading; now I can read. In fact, I love to read. Jesus has even healed my sinuses, which used to hurt so much I'd have to lie flat on my back without moving a muscle for at least half an hour, until the pain went away. I haven't had a shred of sinus trouble in years.

He's made me a whole person. I can forgive now, and I can love. I'm sensitive to other peoples' needs. And that power came from God. It isn't fantasy, and it isn't make-believe. It's real.

I know it. I know that he is real. I'm sure of it because of what he's done for me.

*"As a student I was very, very angry.
I thought that everything everywhere
was wrong. I rejected my religion. My
life was a wreck."*

Christine Elwart

Age 28, high school religion teacher,
married 6 years, 2 children

I WAS IN high school during the Vietnam War, and everybody at that time was talking dissension, activism, militancy. This was after Vatican II, when religious educators had discarded a lot of things, but hadn't replaced them with anything. Everybody just seemed dissatisfied with the way things were.

I was dissatisfied, too. As a student, I was constantly presented with social justice problems, but no one offered any answers. Everyone seemed to be saying, "Things are really rotten in the world, Chris, and you're somehow responsible for it, so you have to do something about it." But no one ever knew what to do.

In the midst of this, I went to South America on an exchange program, where I was exposed for the first time to real hunger and poverty. I worked in the slums, and it was really awful. That experience touched me deeply. I was already upset about things, but by the end of that year I was very, very angry.

Like a lot of kids, I believed "the system" was corrupt. I thought everything everywhere was wrong. I was really looking for answers, but my anger had no outlet. I joined a student organization—a bunch of bitter kids who wanted to do something but didn't know what to do. Then I started drinking and doing all kinds of things that I shouldn't have. I still went to church with my family, but anger became a dominant force in my life.

By then I was intent on just one thing: I was determined to find a way to straighten something, somewhere, out. I was going to help resolve all those social problems. When I entered college, my anger and frustration were just looking for an outlet.

My college, at that time, was called "Hippie Haven," because the counter-culture of the 60's and early 70's permeated everything, and I fell right into it.

Because the people I associated with in the church hadn't been able to answer my questions to my satisfaction, I rejected the church. In fact, I rejected my religion. I became involved in the whole "experience trip": marijuana, hallucinogenics, "speed." Before long, I was living out the whole angry lifestyle, going against nearly everything I had been raised with.

I really was a mess. My life was a wreck. I was angry, frustrated and empty. One thing I remember very distinctly: I didn't like myself anymore, not at all.

I remember thinking that my parents, who were

good people, would die if they knew what I was really like. I was so disappointed in myself. The drugs and the guilt were taking their toll. I hated to be alone. I couldn't even sleep with the lights out any more. Even when the lights were on, I'd wake up frightened. I knew something had gone haywire. I was being destroyed by guilt, pain, anger, and chemicals, but I didn't know what to do. I wanted truth so badly, something to hang my life on, but I didn't know where to look.

By then, I had been living away from home for a year or two, and had run out of money. I couldn't afford to live anywhere else but home, so I finally went back to my family. But when I returned, I found things very different than when I had left.

Before, life at home had always been very confused; there was always a lot of commotion. My mother used to get so upset about that. But when I went home this time, there was a new peacefulness about my mom and dad and about the house itself. I kept watching, saying to myself, "What's going on here?"

When I realized that the house had become a really peaceful place, it made me feel worse, because I still had all this unpeacefulness inside of me. I wasn't a part of the peacefulness they had, so I ended up feeling even more displaced, like I really didn't belong there any more.

One night, about one in the morning, I came home to find my dad and mom waiting up for me. When I saw them, all I could think was, "They found my dope, and here I go. This is trouble!"

They were sitting at the dining room table. My dad

said, "Chris, we want to talk to you about something."
I sat down, and he said, "We don't know what it is,
but we know that you're really unhappy. We know
there's something terribly wrong in your life, and
we'd like to pray with you." I thought, "Pray with
me?" It sounded ridiculous. It caught me completely
off guard. Prayer was totally removed from my life at
that time, so I didn't even know how to respond.

They asked me to sit down. I protested, but did
what they wanted. Then they each took one of my
hands and started to pray out loud. They just talked
with God. They were so sincere about it, and so
convincing in their belief that the conversation they
were having with God was real that I felt like turning
around to see if God might actually be standing
behind me.

But that's all they did; they just prayed for me.
They talked to God and asked him to help me. And all
of a sudden something inside me seemed to break. I'll
try to explain it, but it's not easy to put into words.

It was as if something broke open, and things began
to come out of me, all the bad things, the pain and
guilt and anger. It was a release of some kind, and as I
sensed this release, I started to cry, really hard. I ran
from the table and shouted at my mother, "You can't
love me! You don't know me! I'm a bad person!" But
she followed me and said, "It doesn't matter what
you've done. We accept you, and so does Jesus." And
I thought, "Wow. Does he really?"

In that instant I knew that Jesus Christ was real. All
of a sudden I had no doubt in my mind. I knew he was
real, and I also knew that he was the truth I was
looking so hard for.

After that, my folks asked me if I would go to a prayer meeting at the church with them. They had been going to these meetings but hadn't said anything about it before. So now, of course, I said I would go.

At the first meeting I went to, I thought the people were kind of crazy because of the way they were praying. It was very demonstrative. But at the same time I experienced a lot of love through them, and that was enough to bring me back to another meeting.

At my second meeting, I couldn't stop crying. First of all, I cried because I realized that I'd been afraid to show any thanks to God. So much a part of my self-image had centered on how the drugs and things were supposed to make me a free spirit, but I realized that these things hadn't made me free at all. In fact, the people at the prayer meeting were much freer than I was. The other thing I realized was that I wasn't ready to handle all the love I was experiencing. I was just surrounded by it, and it was so warm and clean, and it had been so long since I felt warm and clean that the whole thing just overwhelmed me. God not only set me free, but he loved me, too.

Today, my whole life has changed. I'm blessed by my marriage and my children. And I love to share with people, especially young people, how much the Lord really cares about them and wants to help them.

My relationship with Jesus is beautiful. He's my deepest friend, someone who cares about me totally. I don't always feel him there in the same intense kind of way, but I know he always loves me. And I love him and am so thankful that he's active in my life.

I'm a different person now. He's made me alive and happy, and I thank him for it again and again.

"I was so lost in college. I was into all kinds of spiritual adventures. I was taking drugs. I really was searching for truth, but I wasn't looking in the direction of Christianity."

Joe Elwart

Age 29, owner of a maintenance service, married 6 years, 2 children

I WAS SO lost in college. I was into all kinds of spiritual adventures, none of them really good. Some things I just dabbled in, others became a big part of my life: psychic associations, transcendental meditation programs, self-enlightenment groups, spiritual societies of various kinds. I was even trying to be a self-taught "I Ching" thinker and to develop in Aquarian Astrology.

Also, I was taking all kinds of drugs. Sometimes I couldn't even think, let alone speak clearly, because I was smoking marijuana every day and dropping pills, mostly hallucinogenics, several times a week.

At the same time, I was always getting involved in philisophical discussions, asking questions like: What is God? What is truth? That kind of thing. I really was searching for the truth, but I wasn't looking in the direction of Christianity.

The fact that Christianity involved having a personal relationship with Jesus Christ wasn't even part of my thinking at the time. I had never even heard of that as a possibility. When I was growing up, Christianity was presented as just another philosophy. I didn't think of Jesus as a living person. In fact, I would turn to him sometimes, in the spiritualism I was getting into, as a power source. But he was never a person as such, only a "white light," an intangible source of protective power that I turned to, because, even then, some of the experiences I was having told me pretty clearly that I needed protection, though I didn't quite understand why.

So nothing that I was into satisfied me. I was empty and unhappy. Then one night my girl friend Chris let her parents pray with her about her own life, and after that she began to change. Later on she went to a prayer meeting and came back very excited. And she kept telling me about all the good things that were happening in her. So I thought, "Well, I'm game to try anything spiritual. I'll go to a prayer meeting too."

I wasn't hit with any big experience, but I really was challenged by it. I felt nervous and uptight about praising God, and had to ask myself, "Why am I, the one who's into the whole free-thinking life-style, so uptight about praising God, when all these straight middle-classers are so free?" So the next week I came back.

At the second meeting, still nervous but wanting to take part somehow, I decided to chant "om." I heard people making prayer requests—"let's pray for this," "let's praise God for that"—so I requested that we chant "om" three times in honor of the Father, Son, and Holy Spirit. Then I took a deep breath and began this long "om."

Suddenly the coordinator of the meeting stood up, right in the middle of my "om," and began to talk about the love of Jesus. Well I thought that was really rude. I was surprised, but I also realized that at least he was trying to be nice about it. He didn't say "Get out of here" or anything like that. But I was still embarrassed. I remember feeling hot and sweaty, but I stuck around.

As soon as the meeting was over, the coordinator came up to me and said, "Don't go away, OK? I'd like to talk with you." So I stayed. A few minutes later he and another guy came up and we began to talk.

I don't remember much of what was said, but I do recall one thing vividly. They asked me, "Do you know what 'om' means?" I said, "Sure. It's an eastern word, and it means 'all, the all of creation,' and in chanting 'om' it puts you in tune and in connection with all that's in creation."

Then they said, "But the 'all' of creation consists not only of God and what is good, but also of what is anti-God and is evil." They went on to say that they believed there was, in Jesus, a way to be in tune only with the good, and that we shouldn't open ourselves to connections with evil at the same time. That made sense to me, because I believed there was evil. In the past I had experienced some terrible, drug-related, spiritual happenings that showed me evil. So what the men from the prayer meeting said rang true. I did want just the good, not the evil.

Though I wasn't a Christian yet, I received some kind of blessing that night. After we finished talking, the men prayed with me, and from that night on my life started to change.

Chris and I continued to attend prayer meetings. We kept hearing about Jesus as a person, Jesus as the truth. People spoke about the love of Jesus and about how he died to break the power of our sins. Slowly I began to change. I was hungry to read the Bible and to pray, to get closer to Jesus. I sensed that this was real, but I still didn't open myself to Jesus all the way, not yet.

A few months later, Chris and I left on a college field project in which we were to travel around the country studying alternate community life-styles. We had made plans to visit five or six different communities as the basis for our course work.

As we were walking out of Chris' house to leave on the trip, her mom mentioned, "If you happen to get to the area around Houston, Texas, there's a Christian community in a church called Holy Redeemer. You might want to stop in and see them too." That's all she said. We thanked her and left.

On the trip, all the stops we had planned began to fall through. Our study project was turning into a disaster. One place said they never made arrangements to let us visit them. Another had to turn us down at the last minute. Without much alternative we found ourselves in Houston looking for Holy Redeemer and thinking, "If this one falls through, the whole report is gone."

Well, it didn't fall through. It was one of the greatest blessings of our lives. Because the other places couldn't take us, we had more time to spend at Holy Redeemer. We stayed in households within the community and experienced the gospel lived out to an extent that we had never seen before. Jesus was shared everywhere, and everything was shared with us. In that context, I was finally set free to give myself, as totally as I knew how, to Jesus. The night before we left to go home, they prayed with us for Baptism of the Holy Spirit. And in my heart I accepted Jesus as the Lord of my life and as my Savior.

Nothing dramatic happened outwardly. But when they were finished praying, I can remember that everything seemed very clean to me. The room seemed clean; even the world seemed clean.

That was seven years ago. Since then, Jesus has changed me in so many ways. Most importantly, he's freed me to love and to receive love.

Because of all the troubles in my family when I was growing up, for example, I was sure that I'd never want to get married or have children. I'd been so badly messed up myself. But Jesus healed me of all that. Chris and I were married and now have two beautiful daughters. And I love them and can care for them. I'm able to assume responsibility for these new lives, and that's the work of God. I could never have done it before.

He's healed me and put me back together. He's made me whole and proved to me again and again that I have found the truth.

"It was easy for me to go to church on Sunday and then turn around and live however I wanted for the rest of the week. In no way was God personal to me."

Hugh Buchanan

Age 30, foreman for a manufacturing plant, married 7 years, 2 children

UNTIL A FEW years ago, I thought that Jesus was pretty much synonymous with the church—the place I went to on Sundays. I was a regular church-goer, but my faith wasn't active. It was easy for me to go to church on Sunday and then turn around and live however I wanted for the rest of the week. I could do that because I thought that God really wasn't looking at me. You know, this is a big world. I went along with the program, but in no way was God personal to me.

My first introduction to Jesus as a real live person came through my wife, Mary. She dragged me to a few prayer meetings at our church. But I held out. I guess I was still "going along with the program," but I didn't let myself get personally involved. During the prayer meeting I'd fade into the part of the church that was empty and just wait for the meeting to end. That way, I kept my distance.

Then Jesus touched me. It was totally unexpected, and it was incredible. He changed my life in a way I never dreamed possible. It happened when Mary and I went to a renewal conference in Kansas City. I had agreed to take her and the kids, but again, I wasn't going to get personally involved. I was determined to hold out.

At the opening meeting there were about 45,000 people. We were in the stadium, and the speaker was really a dynamic guy. And as I sat there, waiting for a chance to fade away, what he said really began to strike me. At one point he said, "I want you to do something. I want you to take your hands and clasp them together tight, like you're holding onto your dearest possessions and you don't want to let them go, because if you open your hands you're going to drop your possessions and lose them forever."

OK, so here I am, squeezing, and he went on talking. He said, "Jesus has given us everything we have. All of our positions, the people we meet, the people we love, our possessions—the whole world. Everything that means anything, he's given to us." Then he said, "Now realize that he's given everything to you, and take your hands, and open them up very slowly, and offer everything back to Jesus."

I was thinking pretty hard by that time, about my family, my home, my position at work. And that's when God really touched me. This guy said, "Now open your hands and offer this to Jesus." I tried to open them but I couldn't bring myself to do it! I forced them open about half way, but I couldn't open them any farther. I just didn't want to do that. I said to myself, "You just can't do it, can you? You can't offer anything back to your Creator, can you?" And as I thought about that, about who I was and what I was really like, I began to open my hands. That was the first time in my life that I ever opened my hands in prayer to the Lord.

After that I don't know what happened. I don't even remember the next couple of minutes. My wife says that all of a sudden she heard "Alleluia!" next to her, and then she heard, "Praise the Lord"" and "Glory to the Lord!" She says that when she turned to look at me, I had my arms straight up in the air with my hands open, and I was smiling, laughing, and praising God. I can remember knowing that he really came to me, and I just wanted to praise and thank him. Jesus said to me at that time, "Hugh, I give you what I give you because I love you. And you can feel free to open your hands. With your hands closed I can't give you any more. But with your hands open, I can give you anything. I can give you my love."

That's when he first touched me. It was so powerful that I felt like I was walking on cloud nine for the rest of the conference. After we got back from Kansas City and unpacked the car and put the kids to bed, I ran down the street in the pouring rain to a friend's house, and I talked to him for forty-five minutes about the things the Lord had done. It was ten o'clock at night, and I didn't even know him all that well, but God had really touched me powerfully, and I've carried that with me to this day.

Whenever I think about where I am now, and

about whether I'm being honest with myself, I think about my hands. I ask myself "Am I closing my hands again?" As a father, I'm tempted to think, "Boy, I've got to put my arms around everything and hold everything in, otherwise it might all fall apart." But I don't have to do that anymore. Now I can hold my hands open.

God has changed me so much. He helps me to see others with a more understanding eye. And it really makes life easier. Instead of looking at the other guy and wondering how I can get even with him, or wondering what he's going to do next, I can look at him and really trust him, and myself, because I trust the Lord.

My focus now is on bringing Jesus into my home. I want to make him the center of our family life; I want my children to learn that Christ is the head of our house, and he's the one who must rule in our lives.

All the while, I know that Jesus and I are getting closer. I realize I've met a terrific new friend, and I'm really excited about all he's shown me and done for me. I never used to read the Bible, either, but now when I read it I think, "That really applies to me!" The other day, for example, I read a passage that talked about Jesus saving two kinds of people. Some were weak and sick and came asking for his help, and he healed them. Others didn't come asking for help. They were too weak, sick, or sinful to know that they needed help. So he had to go and seek out these people. And I know that's how he came and found me.

He didn't just come for people who know they're lame. He came for everybody. He came for me.

Meditation

The Love of God

"May you be able to feel and understand as all God's children should, how long, how wide, how deep, and how high his love really is; and to experience this love for yourselves" (Eph 3:18).

At the heart of each of these encounters with Jesus is the experience of his pure, peaceful, and forgiving love. Notice how consistent that experience is.

The presence of God is always the presence of love, because God *is* love. To encounter the Lord in a personal way is not just to meet up with someone who loves you, but someone who *is* love. To know the Lord is to know something of how long and wide, deep and high love really is, because he is love. He can be nothing else but love.

"We beg you," says Paul, "as though Christ himself

were here pleading with you, receive the love he offers you—be reconciled to God." And when we are, we find that there is really no difference between the two.

To receive the love he offers is to receive him. To receive him is to receive the love he offers. Because God is love, love within love. And his gift to each of us is himself.

"Having seven children and not having a good relationship with God, there were days when I was just in pieces, dancing on the ceiling. My constant cry to God was, 'Why me? What are you doing to me?'"

Barbara Romano

Age 44, homemaker,
married 22 years, 7 children

IT TOOK ME a long time to get to know Jesus—all of thirty-eight years. During those years I never could believe that God really loved me. I was convinced that I was incapable of being loved, or of really loving.

For as long as I can remember, I've been shy and insecure. I never had any self-confidence. As a result, I stored up a lot of anger and resentment inside.

Sometimes I felt that God had a vendetta against me, and I resented him. Having seven children and not having a good relationship with God, there were days when I was just in pieces, dancing on the ceiling. There wasn't a day that passed, for years, when I wasn't filled with anger. My constant cry to God was, "Why me? What are you doing to me?"

These fears and resentments were there for as long as I can remember. When I was a child I was fearful. After I got married and had seven children, it became more difficult for me to handle the situation. At times I thought I just couldn't cope. I was sure I'd go out of my mind if something didn't happen.

All the while I knew my faith was very thin. I was really having trouble and needed something. I was following the rules, but somehow I wasn't really being a Christian. You know, I went to Mass and received the sacraments, but my religion wasn't carried over into the rest of my life. I used to think, "I must be the world's biggest hypocrite. I act one way under a certain set of circumstances and another when there are demands on me to be a Christian." I knew there had to be something more. To be a Christian meant to be like Jesus. But I couldn't figure out how I got from where I was to where he was.

I guess I thought it had to be one of three things. One, somebody wasn't telling me something; two, I wasn't listening hard enough; or three, it was my problem, and I just couldn't expect to get from here to there. These were the only possibilities I could think of, and I'd look at them very seriously and I'd say, "It has to be that somebody isn't telling me something."

All of this reached a head when I was thirty-eight. That's when Jesus entered the picture in a whole new way. I was like the man in the New Testament who sat by the pool every day of his life waiting to be healed by the angel that stirred the water, but whenever he tried to reach the pool, someone else got there first, and the angel healed the other guy. Then

Jesus came along himself and healed the man. That's what I experienced. I had missed out on something all my life. But when I was thirty-eight Jesus just came along and healed me.

One day my best friend said, "Hey, why don't we go to one of those prayer meetings they've started at the church?"

"Well," I said, "it doesn't sound too interesting, but I'll go if you want me to." Actually, I was a little curious about it myself.

When I did go, I wasn't exactly disappointed. I was upset. To see people pray out loud, raise their hands, and hug one another was a shock. It seemed like such a radical way to pray and praise God. They were all so open! My feelings were always in check, so to me this was very radical. In fact, it knocked me flat. I couldn't sleep that night and was upset the whole week. I was sure I would never go back again. But the following week, when my friend asked if I would go, I said, "yes," and I've been going ever since.

I just got drawn back; that's all I can say. Deep down I wanted to return to the meeting. God was there, and he was a loving God. I sensed him, and his love, very strongly.

A few months later, some of the people from the prayer meeting prayed with me for a release of the Holy Spirit in my life. That was the turning point. They prayed for me, and the next thing I knew I was overwhelmed with a sense of God's presence. I was convinced, then and there, that he loved me.

Before, I had doubted God's existence, but now, in the midst of that prayer, I was just engrossed in him. I felt his tremendous love and knew that it was more powerful than anything. I was with God, and would continue to be with him. I knew he was not a God of vengeance, but a God of love and mercy. Everything began to change for me after that. And to this day that love hasn't stopped amazing me.

As I look back over the past five years, I know that the biggest change in me comes from realizing that I am loved. The fact that God loves me continues to dazzle me. And I know that I love God.

There are other important changes he's made in me. To camouflage my own faults, I would often be critical and judgmental of others. It was a defensive thing with me. But I don't need to do that anymore.

My family had always seemed like a burden to me. Now I know they're a great blessing. I can raise the kids differently. I can let them know early in life that Jesus really and truly loves them.

My home is peaceful now. It never used to be. It couldn't be peaceful, because I wasn't peaceful. Now I'm at peace so my kids and my husband can be too.

Before, I was an inch away from a nervous breakdown, but now, with Jesus so close, I feel free. I have an intense love for God, and I don't get flustered, upset, or shook. I'm physically, emotionally, and spiritually healthy.

God has blessed my marriage too. I always doubted that my husband could really love me. Now I know that he does. You see, God has even freed me from that fear. And now I love my husband more than ever.

What else can I say? That's my life now, thanks to Jesus Christ. It's filled with love, and it gets better every day.

"All this time I had resisted going to prayer meetings with my wife, Barbara. I just didn't think they were for me. I liked to go to church by myself and pray quietly."

Sam Romano

Age 48, senior project engineer, married 22 years, 7 children

I GREW UP in a very religious family, knowing who Jesus was. I knew that he had saved me, and I knew something about his life. Yet, as I've come to realize, I never really knew Jesus in a deeply personal way. When I prayed to him, it was like praying to a thing, somehow. It didn't seem like I was really talking to an honest-to-goodness person.

In these last few years, I've come to understand that Jesus lives in me as a real person. I talk with him just as though he's sitting next to me.

Before, I was always trying to do everything myself. If I couldn't do it, nobody could. So I thought it was my fault if the kids were bad, or if the job wasn't going right. Even though I would pray about these things, I always tried to do everything my own way.

Just a few years ago, life started getting rough. In fact, everything seemed to be falling apart.

All this time I had resisted going to prayer meetings with my wife, Barbara. She had begun attending them a couple of years before, but I just didn't think they were for me. For example, I didn't like the idea of praying out loud. I liked to go to church by myself and pray quietly. Even Mass was a very enclosed experience for me. It was never a real "communion," never a group offering or family union.

At any rate, Barbara saw that things were pretty serious with me. I was nervous, withdrawing more and losing confidence. She said to me one day, "Don't you think it's time you tried something new?" So I said, "OK, I'll try your prayer meeting."

As soon as I gave it a try, things began to change. The more I went, the more I enjoyed it. I had intended to just sit back and watch. But as it turned out, I really felt the Lord leading me to become more involved with him, to make a deeper commitment to him. Finally, one day I knew I wanted to say "yes" to God.

It wasn't easy for me to reach that point. I always wanted to be the one in total control of everything. But as soon as I said "yes" to Jesus, even though I was scared, my life began to change in so many good ways.

My circumstances haven't changed; I don't face fewer problems. In fact, I'm involved with more people now than ever before, so I'm probably exposed to more problems. But they don't seem insurmountable anymore. That's what's changed.

God has changed me as a father, too. Before, I was

always very strict. It was important to me that my kids went the right way, and that meant my way. I was the ruler, and my children feared me more than anything else. But since I've come to know the Lord's love, I'm much more able to really love and help the kids. In fact, I have more trust in them now because I place them in God's hands. Every morning I place them in his hands. I don't worry so much about them or come down heavy on them anymore.

The Lord's really changed me as a husband too. He's taught me a lot about what it means to love, so I'm able to love Barbara better now. I want her to be happy more than anything, and I have to admit that wasn't always the case. But now that's all I really want. I'd do anything that would really make her happy.

It's all because of God; he's letting me love more. I look at all the people I pray with and share life with, and there isn't a person that I don't really love. I know that this has to be a work of God, because I don't think it's possible to love so many different people on your own. Yet the more I love, the more my life takes on meaning.

I never dreamed that Jesus would be what he is to me today, or that he would change my life so completely and quickly. He's my brother, my Lord and Savior, and I can't possibly thank him enough.

"Even though I was really unhappy, I didn't look to God for answers. I thought, 'Maybe he's there and maybe he's not. So what?'"

Dennis Hurley

Age 37, high school teacher,
married 17 years, 3 children

THREE YEARS AGO I was really unhappy with my life and my marriage. I thought that life owed me more than I was getting, and my wife took the brunt of this unhappiness. I was a miserable character to live with.

I wasn't really searching for anything, either. Even though I was unhappy, I thought I had it all together. As far as I knew I had as much as there was to have.

I had been raised a Catholic, and as a child, had always had a strong faith. But when I was twenty-two or twenty-three my faith fell apart. I didn't believe in anything anymore. In fact, I was very hostile toward religion. I had become totally disillusioned with the church or any life in God.

So even though I was really unhappy, I didn't look to God for answers. Those few times when God crossed my mind, I didn't feel that his possible existence had much to do with me. I thought, "Maybe he's there and maybe he's not. So what?"

Then one night when I was visiting a friend, he told me about Jesus, and his own life, and about prayer meetings he was attending, and I became curious. I was especially interested because these things were going on in the Catholic Church. It seemed like such a novelty. After our conversation, my friend invited my wife and me to a meeting.

The truth is that I was more interested in the possibility that my wife would benefit from them than I would. I really didn't think I had much to gain from something like that, but I thought that this might smooth out some things for my wife.

The first night we went, the prayer meeting was incorporated into a Mass, which meant a Mass with a whole lot of prayer and praise. Well, I hadn't been to church for years and I was absolutely struck by the love expressed during this Mass. It made a tremendous impact on me.

Though I hadn't expected it, I really felt God's presence. He was so real to me that during the Mass I felt myself starting to cry, and that scared me. I thought, "No. I can't get into this. It's too emotional." So I fought hard against it.

I resisted it, not just for the rest of the night, but for the following week. Even so, I couldn't deny that tremendous sense of love, the strong sense of God's presence that I had experienced. I figured I owed it to myself to take one more look.

I went back to the meetings. And, again, I was confronted by the love that was present. So I started looking deeper. I started to read the Bible and to talk with people and ask questions. I wanted to know how they had found the peace and joy that they had. I asked God, too, for answers. I was particularly struck by something that Jesus said at the Last Supper: "A new commandment I give to you, that you love one another. By this love you have for one another, men will know that you are my disciples." This really struck me now as the answer to everything. It was as if it had been laid out before me, with arrows pointing to it saying, "This is your answer, fella. You are reading your answer."

I knew it was true. The real answer to everything was in the love I experienced that first night. God's answer to me was that I should love him, my wife, and my family; I should let my love out. I couldn't keep everything inside of me anymore.

After that, the love, peace, and happiness I'd been missing gradually became more and more a part of my life.

I began to see myself much more honestly. Before, I had never been able to admit that I was often to blame for my own problems. Now I began to recognize my selfishness, and these self-centered attitudes started to be lifted from me. I prayed steadily, and things changed.

For a time, I struggled to figure out who Jesus was. Was he really God? I used to live on a farm just outside the city. Whenever I wanted to think, I would climb up into the hayloft in the barn. One day I was up there thinking about who Jesus was, and I found a Bible. It wasn't mine, and I had no idea how it got into the loft. But I opened it and read the first thing I came to. I had opened to the passage where the Pharisees ask Jesus: "How can you say these things? How can you talk the way you do? You're not even thirty years old!" And Jesus answers, "Before Abraham was, I am."

My questions about Jesus were cleared up at that moment. He existed before Abraham and was one with the Father. I could really accept him as my Lord and God. I knew he was talking to me through that passage, telling me who he really is. It was as if God had just said, "Listen, Dennis, this is it." His answer just leaped off the page at me.

But the greatest change in my life goes right back to what he let me know that first night at a prayer meeting—his love. He's given me a brand new ability to love and to receive love. I see the whole universe now as filled with the love of God. I was trying to hide from it, but now he's freed me to be a part of it.

I love people that I once thought I could never relate to in any way. Christ has freed me to do that. And because my love for them is real, I see changes in them.

It's all more proof to me that he loves me. And now I just live through proof after proof of that love.

"I was peaceful and happy. I received Communion every day. Then one day our pastor called and said, 'We're starting a prayer group. Why not come?'"

Mildred Howell

Age 55, homemaker, married 32 years, 5 children (one deceased)

ALL MY LIFE I've believed in God. But over the last six years he's let me experience his love in ways that have made a tremendous difference to me, though they're sometimes difficult to describe.

Six years ago I thought that my whole life was in order. Everything was fine. God was not extremely personal to me; he was omnipotent and distant. But he cared very much for me. In fact, I knew he loved me even though he seemed far away.

So I was peaceful and happy. I received Communion every day and was active in the ladies' guild. Then one day our pastor called and said, "We're starting a prayer group. Why not come?"

Because I was interested and didn't want to disappoint the pastor, I went. The group was small, since it had just met for the first time the week before, but I honestly didn't feel at home in it. I don't know why, I just didn't. The way the people prayed seemed so foreign to me.

The week after that I intended to call Father to tell him that I didn't think I belonged at the meeting. I reached for the phone several times but never called. I just couldn't quite do it. Instead, I returned to the prayer meeting, and this time I felt more at home. So the following week I went again. It was during that third meeting that God touched me and let me know that this was where he wanted me.

It was really something. The presence of Jesus simply overwhelmed me. I was immersed in his love, and I couldn't help but cry, but not out of sadness. It was exhileration. I really experienced his love, and that was the beginning of my new relationship with Jesus.

After that I knew my life wouldn't be the same. I realized that the love of God was what life was all about. Today Jesus is the most important person in my life. I love him and know that his love for us is incredibly deep.

He's also enabled me to love others in ways I never could before— especially the aged and the sick. Years ago when I tried to visit convalescent homes I had such a hard time. I felt compassion, but I shuddered at the sickness and helplessness of it all.

Now Jesus has made me feel at home with these people and their suffering. I love them. I see their pain, but I'm not afraid. Because of Jesus' love for them, I can look at them with his eyes. Now I can be with them, hold them, and kiss them no matter what their condition is or what their sores are like. And I know that I really do love them.

The Lord has changed my life because he's a God of love. He *is* love. That's the good news. His love is indescribable, and it's given to everyone, everywhere.

"By the time I was in high school, I was into alcohol; I was into drugs; I had walled myself off completely from my family and their values."

Tom O'Hara

Age 24, student

WAY BACK WHEN I made my first Communion, my relationship with the Lord was a very serious thing to me. I was only in first or second grade and had a very childlike image of God, but he was real to me. I remember that I wanted to respond to him with everything I had.

As I grew up and started to experience more peer pressure, I began to let my faith slide. Then I dropped it all together. I was just doing things to get attention and gain friends, and before too many years I really became something of an outlaw.

I can remember consciously rejecting everything about Jesus Christ because I wanted to be accepted by a certain crowd of people. Not long after that I rejected the value system of my folks and of my earlier education. Then I was into drugs, the whole bit. I thought that if that was all there was, why not go all the way?

So by the time I was in high school, I was into alcohol; I was into drugs; I had walled myself off completely from my family and their values. I wasn't even able to share my questions with them. I couldn't tell them about bad times because I had isolated myself from their values, and I couldn't talk about what I thought were the good times because they all revolved around experiences with drugs and my "doper" friends.

By the time I was in college, I was getting high every day. I was taking a lot of hallucinogenics by then and was totally mixed up.

One night, after I had taken some hallucinogenics, I had an experience of evil that's hard to put into words, but it was a very real and terrible experience. It was only a sensation, but I knew something else was going on besides chemicals. There was a realm to all of this that I hadn't counted on or expected. I was being put into contact with something evil, some personal kind of evil outside of myself. I really felt Satan's presence—a personal, overpowering presence, filled with death, and I knew he hated me.

It was very real and powerful, and I was so frightened that I started groping for God then and there. I realized that I needed him, but my only experience with prayer had been reciting prayers by rote from my prayer book when I was just a kid. So I drove home and rummaged through my old things until I found that prayer book, and I tried to say the prayers but couldn't.

By this time I was really scared. I didn't even know

how to say the Our Father anymore. I felt lost and trapped.

So I cried out, "God, if you're real, you've got to do something. You've got to get me out of this." And God answered me. He didn't send any lightening bolts, but he suddenly gave me a very clear picture of something I had never really taken in before.

I thought about my brother-in-law and my sister, who were both undergoing huge changes in their lives. My brother-in-law's situation hit me especially hard. I had always admired him because he was very intelligent and had been an agnostic. He believed that one religion was as good as another, since none of them were real anyway. Now though, suddenly, he was a committed Christian. He was saying openly that Jesus was real and loved him, and that really hit me hard.

I realized, too, how deeply my sister had accepted Jesus. All of a sudden, my sister was going to prayer meetings, and she was really changing. She was happy. She'd come home from these meetings laughing and excited, bubbling and joyful. And again, the significance of it really hit me.

I had asked Jesus, if he was real, to do something, and he showed me that he was working in people's lives today—right in my own family. He was working like I used to dream he did when I was just a little kid.

I didn't know what to do with it, though, so I didn't do anything right away. I just carried the whole thing with me for awhile. Even though I was unhappy being what I was, I was afraid of becoming a "Jesus freak." I thought that would be too shallow, and not what I needed at all.

Then one night, when I was wrestling with all this, my sister called and invited me to a prayer meeting, so I accepted. And at that meeting, God began to change my life.

I sat in the meeting that night, and I realized how many people around me, including my sister and brother-in-law, had a close relationship with God, and I wanted that. I sat there and I really wanted to pray. But, again, I didn't even know how to pray.

The only thing I could remember were the first prayers I learned as a little kid, and I couldn't even remember the words. I could just remember the sign of the cross. When I was little, my first step to the Lord had always been to make the sign of the cross. So I did that, there at my first prayer meeting. I just made the sign of the cross. I made it as sincerely as I could, and, at that moment, God did something to me. He let me experience his love.

Maybe it happened that way because it was such a simple thing—it was my first step toward the Lord— and he honored it. He gave me a sense of his love that I couldn't deny or fight even if I had wanted. God is love, and as much as I was afraid of becoming known as a "Jesus freak," I knew I couldn't fight that love. It was too powerful.

When I told my friends that I had gone to a prayer meeting, they laughed at me and gave me all the typical college reasons why I shouldn't believe in Jesus: all the anthropology, psychology, sociology, the various theories designed to give you reason not to believe. I knew different because I had experienced God's love. That love was real. They had their theories, but I had something real. I knew that God was real, and I knew that love came from God.

After that, I began to explore Christianity much more seriously. I looked up old friends of mine, a few of whom had already accepted Christ. I saw how their lives had changed. They were laughed at too, but they had something absolutely real. They were convinced and completely sincere.

By that time I was ready to break completely with my old way of life. I knew that Jesus was real and that the things he wanted for me were a lot better than the things the world had to offer. So I asked him to come into my life completely, and he did.

All the destructive things just dropped away. My desire to get high disappeared, and I no longer felt that need for approval from my old circle of friends.

I used to have such a strong need for acceptance among my peers. That's why I began taking drugs. But the Lord let me know that he made me, and I couldn't do anything to improve on his creation. Suddenly I could be who he made me to be, because he gave me the tools I needed: the love, the security, even a group of Christian brothers and sisters to share my new life with.

All of a sudden I understood that by taking all those drugs I was really just running away from real life. And that's what Jesus was offering me—real life.

Now I have tremendous inner peace. I know that God is real, that he's in control, and I'm free from all the burdens I used to carry. It's the direct opposite of the fear I felt when I sensed Satan. God took the chains off me, and I was freed. All the desires, the lusts, all the things the world says are so cool but that were really destroying me, just fell away. I was free to be who God made me to be.

That's the truth that sets us free: God gives us his love completely. He says, "Let me love you." It's like a marriage: the honeymoon is beautiful, but it's also beautiful to live the full life of union, and to grow together. That's where the Lord is with me now. He is my friend, my helpmate, my teacher, my comforter. He's with me wherever I go and whatever I do. God loves me, and that's what's real.

Afterword

THE TESTIMONIES IN this book can't change your life. But if they encourage you to be open, in even the smallest way, to the One "who, by his mighty power at work within us, is able to do far more than we would ever dare to ask or even dream of" (Eph 3:20), then they have been worthwhile.

What I said before is true: the most important discovery we can ever make is to find out with real certainty, through all the doubt, fear, and scepticism that we bring to the question, that Jesus Christ's entering into ordinary lives in personal, powerful, saving ways is not extraordinary at all. It is ordinary.

Jesus invites you to make that discovery now. He is inviting you to know him in this way. He is listening to you, loving you, inviting you now. He wants you to know that this invitation is real, that he is real.

If you already know him, you know that he is always inviting us into a deeper relationship. If you have never been open to Jesus before, he is inviting you to experience a relationship that is utterly unique; to dare to hope again that God will be your God; to know that he is real and that he loves you and will make a difference in your life.

In the last book of the Old Testament the Lord says to his people, "Try me in this. Shall I not open for you the floodgates of heaven, to pour down blessing upon you without measure?" (Mal 3:10). And he is still saying "Try me!"

At the end of the New Testament, in the last chapter, the Lord says, "Let the thirsty one come—anyone who wants to; let him come and drink the water of life without charge" (Rv 22:17).

God has spent all of human history inviting us to try him. Jesus has spent each day of our lives inviting us to try him. He is inviting you now. Speak with him. Listen to him. Be loved by him. Try him.

There is no special prayer or technique. There is only the person Jesus.

"At the favorable time I have listened to you; on the day of salvation I came to your help. Well, now is the favorable time; this is the day of salvation" (2 Cor 6:2).

"Jesus' disciples saw him do many other miracles besides the ones told about in this book, but these are recorded so that you will believe that he is the Messiah, the Son of God, and that believing in him you will have life."

(Jn 20:30-31)